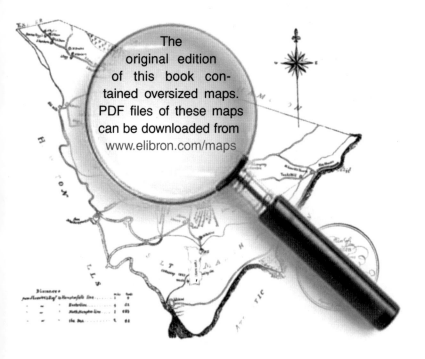

The
original edition
of this book con-
tained oversized maps.
PDF files of these maps
can be downloaded from
www.elibron.com/maps

George Sydenham Clarke

Russia's Sea-Power

Past and Present

or

The Rise of the Russian Navy

Elibron Classics
www.elibron.com

RUSSIA'S SEA-POWER

RUSSIA'S SEA-POWER

PAST AND PRESENT

OR THE

RISE OF THE RUSSIAN NAVY

BY COLONEL

SIR GEORGE SYDENHAM CLARKE

K.C.M.G., F.R.S.

AUTHOR OF "FORTIFICATION," "IMPERIAL DEFENCE," ETC.

WITH MAPS AND ILLUSTRATIONS

LONDON

JOHN MURRAY, ALBEMARLE STREET

1898

Printed by Hazell, Watson, & Viney, Ld., London and Aylesbury.

PREFACE.

FOUR years ago it occurred to me that a historical sketch of the rise of the Russian Navy might be useful, in view of the growing interest displayed in what the authors of the Address of the House of Lords to Queen Anne in 1708 aptly termed " the sea affair." Pressure of other work then prevented me from doing more than accumulate notes bearing upon the subject. Now that public attention is directed to the great naval efforts being made in Russia, and to their connection with the recent supremely important step taken in the

Far East, I trust that the publication of this little book will be deemed opportune.

I cannot claim to have exhaustively treated a large and somewhat intricate subject. I have, however, endeavoured to set forth clearly the main facts connected with the history of the Russian Navy since its inception by Peter the Great, as well as their bearing upon the affairs of Europe during nearly two hundred years. This has involved reference to military operations, and has entailed a degree of condensation by which some of the following pages may seem to be over-weighted. History is not a strong point with the British people ; and although many able writers are now seeking to elucidate the wonderful story of the British Navy, few among us are familiar with the bare outline of the events which have raised the semi-civilised and practically inland State governed by Peter the Great to a dominant position in the affairs of Europe.

In this remarkable development, sea-power has inevitably played a great part; but the process has differed essentially from that which has accomplished the building up of the British Empire.

In the one case, maritime instincts and aptitudes, inherited from seafaring races, combined with almost unrivalled geographical advantages, made the British Islands into a veritable centre of sea-power. The maritime history of England covers a period of nineteen hundred years, and the differentiation of the Royal Navy into a regularised force, apart from a population constantly exercising its natural instincts of fighting on the sea, dates back for four hundred years. That Navy, built up from and supported by national maritime resources in the widest sense of the word, and trained in successive contests with the naval strength of Spain, Holland, and France, succeeded in long years of struggle in establishing its supremacy. Partly by direct conquest, partly by reason of the security which the command of the sea conferred upon a people naturally tending to expand, and wholly by the brilliant achievements of the Royal Navy, the British Empire, as we now understand the phrase, was created.

In the other case, an inland people, as they attained national consolidation, instinctively felt the need of maritime

communications, and forced their way
to the sea, which could be reached only
in the half-frozen Baltic, the doubly
land-locked Black Sea, and the remote
North Pacific. Territorial conquests
from Sweden and from Turkey, together with the subjugation of sparse
tribes owning nominal allegiance to
China, procured for Russia a seaboard
in all respects inferior to that possessed
by other great Powers. Having attained
that seaboard, it was necessary to build
up a navy, which, unlike that of Great
Britain, was thus an artificial creation.
In the Baltic, the new Russian fleet
found itself in conflict with the wasted
navy of Sweden, and later in the South
with the moderately effective forces of
Turkey, already supposed to be tottering
to a fall. Naval experience of some
sort could thus be derived, but such

experience was not comparable to that gained by the British Navy in the stubborn conflict with Holland and the prolonged contest with France and her various allies. In warfare on the high seas, the Russian Navy has as yet played no part ; nor has it in the past directly helped to build up the Empire.

The fundamental difference in the conditions of the development of Great Britain and Russia seems to account, in some measure, for the mutual antagonism which has grown up during the last half of this century. To us, the exercise of all that is implied by maritime power has during hundreds of years been bound up with our national existence. We accept it as a matter of course, and we are, on that account, perhaps unable to realise that another great nation, in proportion to its advance in civilisation and material development, experiences needs precisely similar to those which in our case are abundantly satisfied. In obedience to the dictates of a universal law, the Russian people have sought to obtain an open seaboard. This inevitable movement—the basis of Russian policy for two hundred years—has profoundly influenced the course of events. At the present moment, it is hardly too much to say that the antagonism between Great Britain and Russia is the principal factor in the European situation, supplanting the *vendetta* assumed to exist between France and Germany.

When two nations are mutually estranged, it is generally possible to assign a definite and a sufficient cause.

In the case of Great Britain and Russia, however, the task is by no means easy. Neither commercial nor colonising rivalry at present exists. Nor has there been hitherto any sufficient cause for the antagonism which has frequently threatened to assume an acute form. I have attempted to explain the possible reasons of this antagonism; but I am well aware that the explanation is not wholly satisfactory, since some British sentiment in regard to Russia seems to partake of the nature of that inspired by the personality of Doctor Fell. Sentiment, now as always, plays a far more important part in the affairs of men and nations than reason. It should, however, at least have a basis of fact, and imagination unchecked by a study of events is not a safe guide. The expansion of Russia has conformed to a universal law, and up to the present time it is impossible to discover any violation of territory which Great Britain has ever desired to possess or over which we have any conceivable claim. No substantial grievance against Russia exists at this moment.

There has always been a body of opinion in this country in favour of seeking a direct agreement with Russia, and the present Prime Minister has explicitly stated that our policy in 1854-55 and in 1878 was founded upon a fallacy. There is, however, no clear sign of a definite change. Russia has, in the past, been frequently our ally, and has proved more satisfactory in that capacity than some other Powers. The Russian Navy has been largely the creation of British seamen. Early in the present century, a strong sympathy with the Russian people was manifested in this country. In these circumstances, it is not easy to believe that, with Russia alone of all great Powers, a direct understanding is unattainable.

One thing at least is certain. The policy of seeking to stem the advance of Russia by diplomatic notes and by exhibitions of irritability has absolutely failed. Territory in regard to which we are prepared to accept no responsibilities cannot reasonably be denied to the occupation of another Power. Undefined spheres of influence have no sanctity. In the Far East, therefore, our course is plain. We have, while there is yet time, to define in the clearest terms the territory in which we intend no other influence to be established—the territory the violation of which we should resist with the whole strength of the Empire. Russia and other Powers would then know where they stand, and war, if it should be forced upon us, would be waged in a cause which every member of the British family could comprehend. Fate has, however, ordained that Asiatic dominion should be shared mainly by two great nations. There is ample room for both, and could they attain to a reasonable measure of mutual understanding, fairer hopes of peace and of progress would dawn upon the world.

LONDON, *June* 1898.

NOTE.—My best thanks are due to the Hon. T. A. Brassey for permitting the reproduction from the *Naval Annual* of the diagrams of the *Rurik*, *Sissoi Veliky*, and *Tria Sviatitelia*.

CONTENTS.

CHAPTER I.

CHAPTER II.

CHAPTER III.

CHAPTER IV.

CHAPTER V.

CHAPTER VI.

CHAPTER VII.

CHAPTER VIII.

CHAPTER IX.

FIGURES.

MAPS.

RUSSIA'S SEA-POWER

PAST AND PRESENT;

OR,

THE RISE OF THE RUSSIAN NAVY.

———•———

CHAPTER I.

EARLY HISTORY—WARS OF PETER THE GREAT.

L ESS than two hundred years ago
Archangel was the one seaport
of Russia, and thither large fleets of
British and Dutch merchantmen annually
found their way. When Peter the
Great ascended the throne in 1689,
the Baltic was almost a Swedish lake,
the Black Sea Turkish, the Caspian

Persian. The struggle for a seaboard which then began has since been the ruling motive of Russian policy, and has already graven deep marks upon the history of nations. " We work," wrote Peter, when on his western travels, to the patriarch Adrian, " to effectually conquer the art of the sea, in order that, on our return to Russia, being completely instructed, we may be victorious over the enemies of Christ." Behind the movement inaugurated by Peter lay irresistible natural forces, which sooner or later must have come into play.

The national consolidation which began under Jaroslaf in the eleventh century was first checked by civil wars, and then shattered by the wave of Tartar invasion, which, engulfing all Russia except Novgorod and the territories of the North-west, extended

into Moravia and Silesia. Before the
end of the fifteenth century, the heavy
yoke of the Tartars had been broken,
and Ivan III. had formed a new grouping of the Russian States. Henceforth
Moscow, which since the conquest of
Constantinople by Mahomet II. had been
the metropolis of the Eastern Church,
became also the capital of a great
Muscovite principality. Wars with
Lithuania, Poland, and the Tartar
khanates added territory to the domains
of the Grand Dukes of Moscow, and
in 1547 Ivan IV. assumed the title of
Tzar. The important conquests of
Kazan and Astrachan followed, pointing
out the way into Asia; but in 1572
Moscow was burned by the Tartars of
the Crimea, and the western wars of
Ivan IV. were generally unsuccessful.

The Muscovite dynasty ended with
Feodor Ivanovitch in 1598, and the

death of the Boyar Tzar, Boris Godonoff, in 1605, was followed by a period of acute civil dissension, which led to a Polish occupation of Moscow. A national movement—the first worthy of the name which Russian history records —saved the situation. Minin and Pojarski, whose names are commemorated in armoured cruisers, obtained the capitulation of the Polish garrison, and in 1613 a national assembly elected Michael Romanoff to the vacant throne. A war with Sweden, several Polish wars, and a serious Cossack revolt marked the remainder of the seventeenth century ; but the organisation of the Empire progressed, and under the Romanoffs Western influences began to assert themselves.

During centuries the ships of England, France, Spain, Holland, and Portugal had carried the commerce

of their countries across the world.
In far earlier days, Phœnicians, Greeks,
Romans, Carthaginians, and Norsemen
had scoured the seas.   Great sea fights
had been lost and won; the art of
naval warfare had made striking progress, and maritime operations had
powerfully influenced the development
of nations.   The training, political and
moral, which a people derives from
contact with the sea—a training which,
far more than any other, impresses
itself upon national character—was
wholly wanting to Russia in the days
of her youth.   If the United States
had been developed from the interior,
the original germ having arisen out
of a grouping of Indian tribes roaming
the plains of Nebraska, a parallel to
Russian expansion might be found.
But the races which have peopled
North America, like those which created

England, moved inwards from the coasts, carrying with them the instincts of the sea. The difference of conditions is supremely important, and goes far to explain the relatively slow progress of Russian civilisation.

A great inland State, growing conscious of its power, must inevitably seek outlets to the sea, and to a natural movement the peculiar genius of Peter the Great supplied a sudden impulse. He clearly saw that, in order to become a great Power, Russia needed seaports and a fleet. Turning his attention first to the South, he attempted the siege of Azof, and failed, since the Turks, in command of the sea, were able to keep open communications. Nothing daunted, Peter imported artillery officers from Austria and Holland, engineers from Prussia, an admiral from Venice, and, collecting twenty-six thousand workmen,

he set about building a fleet of galleys
and boats on the banks of the Don.
Blockaded by land and sea, Azof fell
in 1696. It was a small beginning,
and in 1711 the place was restored
to Turkey; but this success, mainly
due to the impromptu flotilla, gave an
impetus to Peter's naval aspirations.

The capture of Azof was the dawn
of a new era in Russian history, and the
opening move of a new national policy,
which soon brought the inland Empire
into contact with the maritime Powers.
Azof, situated at the inner extremity of
a narrow gulf of a trebly land-locked
sea, was not a favourable outlet for
maritime expansion, and the Russian
flotilla could not hope to contend with
the Turkish fleet. Peter's thoughts
were, therefore, soon drawn to the
Baltic, and primarily to the head of
the Gulf of Finland.

The end of the seventeenth century had its Holstein question, which served as a pretext for a coalition against the young King of Sweden. In 1698, an alliance was concluded between Denmark and Saxony, which was joined by Poland and Russia. England and Holland ranged themselves on the side of Sweden, and by an accident of international politics Peter's nascent ambitions were thus early opposed by this country. By Oxenstiern, the Chancellor of Sweden, these ambitions were clearly realised. " If once the Tzar obtains a port on the Baltic," he wrote to Charles XII., " he will hold it come what will." In June 1700, a fleet of twelve line-of-battle ships, under Sir George Rooke, with thirteen Dutch vessels, arrived at Gothenburg, and, being joined by the Swedes, neutralised the Danish squadron, enabling Charles

to land an army on the shores of
Zealand and to threaten Copenhagen.
The Holstein difficulty having been
composed, the British admiral had no
further orders, and, driven to abandon
the idea of attacking the Danish capital,
Charles concluded peace with Denmark,
and determined to carry on single-handed
the war against Russia, Saxony, and
Poland.   Peter had already invaded
Ingria, and was besieging Narva when
Charles landed.   Collecting his force
at Wesenburg, the King attacked the
Russian lines of contravallation on
November 20th, 1699, winning a brilliant
victory over greatly superior forces.
This was the first considerable battle
between the Swedes and the Russians,
whose troops, deserted by their Tzar
on the eve of the action, showed to
little advantage.   In 1701, Charles had
more than sixty thousand men on the

southern coasts of the Baltic. On July
8th, he defeated a Saxon-Russian army
at Riga, and occupied Courland. The
kingdom of Poland, shrunk from its
former dimensions, was already tottering to a fall, when Charles XII. started
on the astounding series of adventures
which ended in disaster at Pultowa.
Utilising the Swedish command of the
Baltic, he might have effectually checked
the designs of the Tzar, in which lay
real danger to his country. Swedish
statesmen viewed with alarm the proceedings of the impracticable hero, and
urged peace with Poland and Saxony.
William III. of England, who had
organised a grand alliance of neutral
Powers to curb the ambitions of Louis
XIV., sent wise counsels ; but Charles
was unmoved, and the practical result
of his wonderful campaigns in the heart
of Europe was to drain the strength of

Sweden and to further the projects of the Tzar. Left to their own resources, the Baltic provinces of Sweden were unable to defend their long frontier against invasion, and in 1702 the Russians overran Ingria and Livonia, and captu ed Nöteburg, now Schlüssel-burg. Nyen, at the head of the Gulf of Finland, fell the following year ; the Neva became a Russian stream, and St. Petersburg was founded. In 1704, Dorpat and Narva were taken. In every case Peter instantly turned to account the waters rendered available, and on Lake Ladoga, the Neva, and Lake Peipus ships were rapidly built. In 1702, he had paid a flying visit to Archangel, launched two small frigates, and laid the keel of a 26-gun vessel. In August, a large fleet of English and Dutch ships arrived at this port under convoy. In the same

year, a Swedish vessel was taken on Lake
Peipus, and in 1703 two others were
captured in the Neva, while on Lake Ladoga the new navy successfully asserted
itself. By the end of 1710, the Baltic
provinces of Sweden were in the hands
of the Russians, and Riga had fallen.

While the naval projects of the
Tzar thus prospered in the North, a
severe check was administered in the
South. The brief Russo-Turkish war
of 1711, which Charles XII. had striven
to promote, ended ignominiously on
the banks of the Pruth, where the
Russian army was surrounded and
might easily have been destroyed by
the Grand Vizier. Peter, acting on the
advice of the Tzarina, saved himself
by offering terms—and money. Azof
was restored to the Sultan, and the
Russian fleet was destroyed. The
Turko-Venetian war, which began in

the following year, gave a fresh stimulus to the Turkish navy. The Swedish cause was now visibly declining, and Charles lingered in the South till September 1714, attempting to govern his distracted country from the neighbourhood of Adrianople! Meanwhile, in May 1713, a combined Russian expedition, under Admiral Apraxine, with Peter as second in command, took Helsingfors and Abo, on the northern shore of the Gulf of Finland, and routed a force of raw Swedish and Finnish levies under Armfeldt at Storkyro. This was the first over-sea operation of Russia, and the following year witnessed her first real naval action, when Peter, with thirty ships of the line, defeated a greatly inferior Swedish force off the island of Aland, capturing four ships of the line, four frigates, and six galleys. The anniversary of the action, known as that of Hangö Udd, was celebrated by Peter on board a British flagship in the following year. Thus rapidly had the development of the Russian Baltic fleet progressed.

In 1715, Denmark and Prussia joined Russia, Saxony, and Poland against the Swedes. Stralsund fell in December, and Charles XII., narrowly escaping capture by the Danish cruisers, returned to his kingdom after an absence of fifteen years.

Great Britain, either acting in accordance with a policy recently imported by George I., or genuinely aggrieved by the action of Swedish cruisers, had in June sent a squadron of eighteen sail of the line under Sir John Norris into the Baltic. A combined fleet—British, Dutch, Russian, and Danish—cruised under the personal command of the Tzar, whose naval aspirations must have

been supremely gratified by this unique
honour. In 1717, Sir John Norris, for
whom Peter had conceived a great
admiration, returned to the Baltic, pre-
venting any action on the part of the
Swedish navy. In the following year,
Charles XII., who had invaded Norway,
was killed in the trenches before
Frederickshald. British policy in the
Baltic now underwent a marked change,
and an Anglo-Swedish alliance was
concluded. In 1719, Sir John Norris
again sailed for the Baltic, joining the
Swedish squadron in September, and
the Russians, who were harrying the
coasts of Sweden, retired to Revel. In
the following year, a similar demonstration was made, and Sir John Norris succeeded in negotiating a treaty between
Sweden and Denmark, while Prussia
also made peace. No naval hostilities occurred, since the Russian fleet declined

action, while difficulties of navigation hampered the Allies.

In 1720, the northern war, which had lasted twenty-two years, came to an end, and its main result was the firm establishment of Russia on the Baltic. The continental campaigns of Charles XII., however glorious to the Swedish arms, had proved ruinous to the nation. The population decreased more than eleven per cent.; the mercantile marine sank from seven hundred and seventy-five to two hundred and nine vessels; the powerful navy, which might have successfully opposed the projects of the Tzar and effectually aided the defence of the Baltic provinces, was reduced to dependence upon allies. Russia had obtained a seaboard extending from Viborg on the north of the Gulf of Finland to the head of the Gulf of Riga, and had built a new capital on the

Neva, guarded by the fortifications of Cronstadt. In the South, the expansion had so far been less successful. The coast-line of the Caspian for three hundred and fifty miles, from the Ural to the South-west, including Astrachan and the estuary of the Volga, was now Russian; but a belt of Turkish territory surrounded the Sea of Azof and embraced the mouth of the Dnieper.

The first period of Russia's march to the sea had brought her into direct conflict with Sweden and Turkey, Powers separated by the breadth of a continent, but confronted by a common danger, which had sent Swedish troops to the banks of the Danube. At the same time, by reason of the exigencies of the Elector of Hanover, rather than from any prescience of a later policy, Great Britain had been brought into opposition to the rising naval Power of the North.

CHAPTER II.

OPERATIONS IN THE BALTIC—FALL OF
PEREKOP—WAR OF AUSTRIAN SUC-
CESSION—SEVEN YEARS' WAR.

IN 1725, Peter the Great died, and was
succeeded by the Tzarina, Catharine I.
Russia, now thoroughly established as
a European State, was suspected of
intrigues with the courts of Vienna and
Madrid. A second quadruple alliance
—Great Britain, France, Prussia, and
Denmark—having been arranged, Sir
Charles Wager, with twenty ships of
the line, one frigate, two fireships,
and a hospital-ship, was sent into the
Baltic in 1726. A Danish squadron
joined the British admiral off Bornholm,

and a Russian force of sixteen sail, under Admirals Apraxine, Gordon, and Saunders, was reported to be at Cronstadt. Vice-Admiral Gordon, however, informed the Tzarina that his fleet was unable to risk an action, and civilities were exchanged, the British squadron returning home in October, while the Russians began to fortify themselves at Revel. In 1727, Sir John Norris sailed for the Baltic, and anchored at Copenhagen on May 12th, causing " dejection to the Russians." With the death of George I. the long series of naval demonstrations ended, and for many years no British fleet seems to have entered the Baltic.

The death of Augustus II. of Poland in 1733 involved a new European war. A Russian army under Lacy marched on Warsaw, and Stanislaus, the son-in-law of Louis XV., fled to Danzig, which was besieged by sixty thousand Russians, Saxons, and Poles under Münnich. A French fleet of sixteen sail entered the Baltic, and in May disembarked three regiments at Danzig. A further reinforcement of fifteen hundred men arrived in the following year under convoy of two ships of war, but could not be admitted on account of the dearth of provisions. The Russian fleet under Admiral Gordon at length appeared on the scene, and Danzig surrendered.

The year 1736 saw the outbreak of a new Russo-Turkish war in prosecution of the aims of Peter the Great. The famous lines of Perekop were forced by Münnich at the end of May, and Azof fell to Lacy on June 29th. Oczakoff, at the mouth of the Dnieper, was taken by the Russians on July 13th, 1737, and unsuccessfully besieged by the Turks during October and

November. On August 9th and
10th, actions were fought between the
Russian Don flotilla under Admiral
Bredal and the Turkish Azof squadron.
The Russian vessels were drawn close
in shore under the protection of an
extemporised battery, and the Turks
suffered some loss. In the vain belief
that the end of the Ottoman Empire
was at hand, Austria entered into the
war, and after failing completely in
three campaigns made peace with the
Sultan. The Russians were, however,
generally successful, and after inflicting
a severe defeat on the Turks, Münnich
occupied the fortress of Choczin, on the
Dniester, on August 30th, 1739. The
Empress Anne, weary of the war, re-
jected an offer of aid from Nadir Shah,
just returned from his march to Delhi,
and concluded peace at Belgrade in
October. The Russian Empire gained

an increase of territory on the side of the Ukraine; Azof and Taganrog were demolished; but the results of the war were inconsiderable, and the Euxine was still a Turkish lake.

The deaths of the Emperor Charles VI., of Frederick William of Prussia, and of the Empress Anne in 1740 led to the War of the Austrian Succession. On January 1st, 1741, Frederick II. entered Breslau, the capital of Silesia, and the European Powers regrouped themselves. France, opposing Maria Theresa, who was supported by Russia, found means to embroil Frederick of Sweden, who declared war on July 12th. A fleet was equipped to blockade the Russian ports in Livonia, and eleven thousand Swedes advanced against Wilmanstrand, where they were defeated by a superior Russian force under Lacy. In December, Count

Löwenhaupt, with the main Swedish
army, moved on Viborg. A revolution
at the Russian Court, directed against
German influence, placed Elizabeth, the
daughter of Peter the Great, on the
throne ; but, after a short armistice,
the war was renewed, and Löwenhaupt
surrendered to Lacy near Helsingfors.
On May 18th, 1743, a combined
expedition under Lacy sailed from
Cronstadt for Helsingfors, and proceeded to seek the Swedish fleet at
Tweermunde. The Russian squadron
of seventeen sail of the line, with six
frigates and a large galley force, was
ordered by Lacy to attack ; but no
anxiety for action was manifested on
either side, and after the exchange of
a few shots the fleets separated. In
August, peace was concluded. In 1746,
the British Government undertook to
subsidise Russia, who was to place

thirty-seven thousand men and forty
galleys at the disposal of the Allies.
These troops might apparently have
been transported by sea, and enabled
to take part in the campaign in Holland ;
but the arrangement led to nothing, and
after a march of seven hundred miles
the Russians wintered in Moravia, returning home when the war ended with
the Treaty of Aix la Chapelle in 1748.

The outbreak of the Seven Years'
War brought about a conflict between
Russia and Prussia. The Tzarina
Elizabeth sent a squadron of fifteen sail
to blockade the Prussian ports and to
bombard Memel, which surrendered to
a land force under Fermor ; but after
defeating Lewald at Gross Jägersdorf,
the Russians recrossed the Niemen.*
In 1758, Fermor again invaded Prussia,

* An illness of Elizabeth is said to have been
the cause of the retirement.

occupied Königsberg, and laid siege to Custrin on the Oder, which was relieved by Frederick the Great in August. Defeated at Zorndorf, Fermor marched into Pomerania, where he failed to take Colberg, which was needed as a port of supply. In 1758, the Russians won the battles of Züllichau and Kunersdorf, subsequently retiring to Poland for want of provisions. In 1760, a Russian fleet of twenty-seven vessels, under Admiral Mishukoff, with a land force of fifteen thousand men, failed in an attempt on Colberg; but in October Berlin was bombarded and occupied for four days by a Russo-Austrian army, which retired on the approach of Frederick. In the following year, a Russian fleet of forty sail, subsequently joined by a Swedish squadron, blockaded and bombarded Colberg, which was at the same time besieged by land. On December 16th,

Colberg fell, and a new line of supply was opened to the Russian armies.

The death of Elizabeth on January 5th, 1762, saved Frederick the Great. Peter III. at once ceased hostilities, and joined his forces with those of the King of Prussia. On July 9th, a revolution at St. Petersburg placed the Tzarina Catharine on the throne ; but, although Russian policy was again temporarily reversed, no active measures were taken, and the last battle of the Seven Years' War was a Prussian victory over the Austrians at Freyberg.

The great European conflicts of 1740-48 and 1756-63 involved naval operations in many seas. Great Britain and France, preoccupied with the struggle for colonial dominion, did not employ their ships in the Baltic, and the Russian fleet at the outbreak of the War of the Austrian Succession numbered at least fifty vessels, subsequently in creased. By reason of the decadence of Sweden there was no force capable of contesting the command of the sea, but the results obtained were inconsiderable. The Russian squadron appeared on the coasts of Prussia, but did not materially aid the land campaigns, and the possible uses of a navy do not seem to have been realised.

CHAPTER III.

WITH the accession of Catharine II. a
new period of expansion began. On
the death of Augustus III. in 1764
Russian influence placed Poniatowski on
the throne of Poland, and on the outbreak of the insurrection in 1768 Russian
troops stormed Cracow. In October
of the same year Catharine declared
war with Turkey, and in 1769 a Russian
squadron under Alexis Orloff was sent
from the Baltic to the Mediterranean.
This was a somewhat risky experiment,

and the ships, after many mishaps, arrived in the Channel in bad condition, "notwithstanding the assistance of some English officers and pilots." * After refitting at Portsmouth the squadron proceeded to Port Mahon, where it arrived "shattered and sickly. The same kind offices being, however, repeated, and the same powerful and masterly assistance which characterises the English nation in everything relating to maritime affairs being again freely given, the ships were put in as good condition as the state they were in could admit of, and the men . . . recovered their health very fast." †

The new Russian departure was differently viewed by the Mediterranean Powers, who placed restrictions on the use of their ports, while Venice altogether excluded the new arrivals

* *Annual Register*, 1769.　　　† *Ibid.*

and fitted out a fleet to guard the Adriatic. In February 1770, the Russian squadron moved on to the Levant, where Orloff succeeded, by issuing manifestoes, in arousing a revolt in the Morea, occupied Navarino, and attacked Patras, Modon, and other places on the coast-line. The intervention of Russia proved disastrous to the Greeks, whom she compromised. The available landing force was too small to obtain any permanent success, and on the arrival of Turkish and Albanian troops the revolt was crushed with great bloodshed, the Russians retiring to Navarino and soon abandoning the Morea altogether. " The fleet," wrote Orloff to Catharine, is " not worth a pinch of salt. . . . My hair stands on end as I think of these things. If we had to do with any but Turks, there would soon be an end of the fleet." In

April, Rear-Admiral Elphinston arrived
from Cronstadt with reinforcements,
after refitting at Portsmouth, and in
May the Turkish fleet appeared in the
Levant. After "some engagements of
no great consequence," the Russian
squadron of ten ships of the line, with
five frigates, under Admiral Spiridoff,
encountered fifteen Turkish ships of the
line, with galleys and small craft, at
anchor between the island of Chio and
the mainland. Here an indecisive
action was fought on July 5th, in which
the two flagships were laid alongside,
and, taking fire, blew up. "The commanders and principal officers on both
sides were mostly saved, but the crews
were nearly totally lost." * At nightfall
the Turks cut their cables, and in
opposition to the wishes of the more
experienced officers ran into the Bay of

* *Annual Register,* 1770.

Tchesmé, where, " huddled together like birds in a net," * they were blockaded by the Russians. On the 6th at midnight, four fireships prepared by Admiral Elphinston were taken into the bay by Lieutenants Dugdale and Mackenzie, the operation being covered by Commodore Greig with four ships of the line and two frigates. The Russians, who were unaccustomed to service of this nature, " showed great backwardness " † ; but Dugdale, though deserted by his crew, succeeded in grappling a Turkish vessel, and set fire to his ship. In five hours the whole fleet, except one 62-gun vessel and a few galleys, was destroyed.

The Russians, now masters of the Levant, blockaded the Dardanelles, interrupted Turkish trade, and besieged the Castle of Lemnos, where they were defeated by Hassan Bey. The Greek

* *Annual Register*, 1770. † *Ibid.*

insurrection had miserably failed, and the revolt of Ali Bey in Egypt, also promoted by the appearance of the Russians, was suppressed in 1773. The Turkish navy made no attempt to retrieve the disaster of Tchesmé, and the Russians, whose ships were in bad order, and whose small force of troops was nearly exhausted, could effect nothing except occasional descents upon unimportant places on the seaboard. The war practically degenerated into piracy.

The great naval enterprise of Catharine II. had spent itself, and such success as it had obtained was entirely due to Great Britain. By the aid of British ports and British officers the Russian squadron reached the Levant. To British officers was due the destruction of the Turkish fleet. The name of Tchesmé is now borne by a

Russian battle-ship; but the fact that
the victory thus commemorated was
due to Elphinston, Greig, Dugdale,
and Mackenzie is altogether forgotten.
Whether originating in the friendship
of Peter the Great with Sir John Norris,
or suggested by the prestige of the
British navy, the practice of obtaining
officers from this country had steadily
grown.   Under Catharine II. the number of such officers, largely of Scotch
descent, was considerable; and when, in
1788, Paul Jones was appointed a rear-
admiral in the Russian service, sixty
are said to have resigned their com-
missions.   Among the earliest importa-
tions was Lord Duffus, who in the
Advice frigate fought a gallant action
with eight French privateers off Yar-
mouth in June 1711.   Carried to Dun-
kirk as a prisoner, he became involved
in the rebellion of 1715, was attainted,

and after being released from the Tower was made an admiral by Peter the Great. Sir Samuel Greig, after seeing service at Quiberon Bay, before Brest, and at Goree, joined the Russian navy as a lieutenant, became rear-admiral after the action at Tchesmé, and was afterwards governor of Cronstadt. His son, Alexis Samuelovich, was made a midshipman at birth in 1775, and won great distinction in the Turkish war of 1827-29, afterwards devoting himself to the organisation of the navy and the development of the Black Sea fleet. A grandson showed great gallantry during the siege of Sebastopol. Elphinston joined as a rear-admiral in 1769, and afterwards returning to England commanded the *Magnificent* in Byron's action off Granada in July 1779, and in the battle between Rodney and de Guichen in April 1780. In 1788,

Captain Sir Frederick Thesiger became a Russian officer, and won laurels in fighting the Swedes, who were assisted by Sir Sidney Smith. The roll is a long one, and the Russian navy may almost be said to be the creation of British seamen.*

On land, except in Bulgaria, the Turkish war was an almost unbroken success for the Russian arms. Bender was taken in September 1770, and the Crimea was overrun in the following year, Balaclava alone holding out. In 1773, the first partition of Poland, originated by Frederick the Great, was accomplished. In the same year, the Russians took Turtukai, and advanced to Varna, where they were repulsed, and failing

* The close connection between the British and Russian navies seems to have existed to a later date, and a Russian lieutenant was wounded on board H.M.S. *Conqueror* at Trafalgar.

before Silistria they recrossed the Danube. The war ended with the Peace of Kainardji, signed on July 21st, 1784, which gave to Russia Kinburn, Kertch, Yenikale, and the district between the Dnieper and the Bug, confirmed her possession of Azof and Taganrog, opened the Bosphorus and Dardanelles to her mercantile marine, and prepared the way for the formal annexation of the Crimea nine years later. As the general result of the war, Catharine, following in the steps of Peter the Great, firmly established herself on the shores of the Black Sea and the Sea of Azof. The Russian navy, under British auspices, had found the way to the Mediterranean, and Russian frigates had anchored before Constantinople.

CHAPTER IV.

THE "ARMED NEUTRALITY"—NAVY IN
BALTIC AND MEDITERRANEAN—RUSSO-
TURKISH WAR—RUSSO-BRITISH ALLI-
ANCE—ALIENATION OF THE TZAR
PAUL—NELSON IN THE BALTIC.

IN 1775, the War of American Independence began, involving Great
Britain successively with France, Spain,
and Holland. The British navy, the
state of which had evoked severe
censures in Parliament in 1771, was
overtaxed, with the necessary result of
general unsuccess. In 1780, Catharine
abandoned the "northern system," and
drew closer to Austria, and afterwards

to France. The "Armed Neutrality"—
Russia, Prussia, Austria, Sweden, and
Portugal—was formed for the protection
of neutral rights ; but, on account of
the great infusion of British officers,
the Russian navy was not in a position
to undertake hostilities against this
country, and the outbreak of a new
Russo-Turkish war in 1787 led to a
fresh grouping of the Powers. Catharine made naval preparations on a great
scale. A fleet of eighteen ships of the
line, with numerous frigates and small
craft, was fitted out under Admiral Greig
for the Mediterranean, and in the Black
Sea the Prince of Nassau commanded
a powerful flotilla. The Mediterranean
expedition was coldly regarded by the
Powers ; Genoa alone offered the ser-
vices of her ports, and the undertaking
of certain British merchants to provide
eighteen vessels for the transport of

stores was frustrated by the action of
the British Government.   Meanwhile,
Catharine concluded an alliance with
Austria and Denmark, and declared war
with Gustavus III. of Sweden.   Thus
the Baltic again became the scene of
naval conflicts.   On July 17th, 1788,
Greig, with seventeen ships of the line,
engaged the Duke of Sudermania, with
fifteen ships of the line and four 40-gun
frigates, off the island of Hoogland.
The action was indecisive, and some of
the Russian captains appear to have
behaved badly ; but Greig, quickly refitting and being reinforced, attacked
the Swedes at Sveaborg, and captured
a ship of the line.   In 1789, Gustavus,
secured by British intervention against
Denmark, made new naval efforts.
The Prince of Nassau, who succeeded to
the command of the Baltic fleet on the
death of Admiral Greig, defeated an

inferior Swedish squadron near Rogens-
alm on August 25th. On May 13th,
1790, the Duke of Sudermania made
a gallant but ill-advised attack upon the
Russian squadron in the fortified port
of Revel, and was repulsed with the
loss of two vessels. On the 15th, the
King of Sweden attacked Fredericks-
ham with his galley fleet, destroying
a number of small craft, together with
docks and large quantities of naval
stores. The Swedish navy was, however, no match for the Russians. On
June 3rd, the Duke of Sudermania
fought an indecisive engagement with
the Cronstadt division, and the Revel
squadron of thirteen ships of the line
under Admiral Tchitchagoff arriving on
the following day, the situation appeared
desperate. The Duke, however, succeeded in extricating his command, and
reached the island of Bjorno, where he

was joined by the King with the galley fleet. The Swedes now undertook a hopeless attack on Viborg, where they were caught by Tchitchagoff, and heavily defeated on July 3rd and 4th, losing three ships of the line, a frigate, and sixty-six galleys and small craft, and seven thousand men. On July 9th and 10th, further actions were fought in Svenska Sound, the Russians being defeated with some loss. Many British officers were engaged on both sides ; Sir Sidney Smith rendered great service to the Swedes, and saved the King from imminent capture by Captain Dennison, commanding the *Venus* frigate.

The resources of Sweden were, however, nearly exhausted ; on August 14th peace was signed, and Catharine was able to bring her undivided energies to bear against Turkey.

The naval operations in the South

were of small importance. The Russians were not yet able to contest the command of the Black Sea, and the Turks were not well provided for fighting in shoal waters. In the Liman estuary several engagements occurred, and on June 7th, 1788, the Russian flotilla, under the Prince of Nassau, covered by the guns of Kinburn, inflicted a severe repulse upon a Turkish force of light vessels, galleys, and ships' boats. " Rear-Admiral " Paul Jones was present, but took no part in the fighting. The Prince of Nassau afterwards co-operated in the siege of Oczakoff, which was captured by Potemkin on November 17th. In the following year, the Austrians gained a victory on the Sereth ; Loudon occupied Gradisca on June 20th, and Belgrade on September 12th ; while on July 31st the Prince of Coburg and Suwarroff defeated the Seraskier near Focsani. On September 22nd, the Russo-Austrian forces routed the Grand Vizier's army at Rimerik in Wallachia; and Potemkin, defeating Hassan Pasha near Bender, occupied Ackerman at the outlet of the Dniester, and Kilia at the northern mouth of the Danube. In 1790, the Austrians were defeated near Giurgevo, and concluded a separate peace on July 27th. Suwarroff, supported by a squadron of galleys sent up the Danube, attacked Ismail, which was stormed on December 25th, and the Russian troops advanced to the Balkans. Further fighting occurred in Bulgaria in 1791, and the Russians invaded the Kuban, and defeated a Turko-Circassian force near Anapa. At Galatz on August 11th were signed the preliminaries of a peace which was concluded at Jassy on January 9th, 1792. Russia retained

Oczakoff and the country between the Bug and the Dnieper ; but Potemkin had died on October 15th, 1791, and Catharine's project of creating for him a kingdom out of Moldavia, Wallachia, and Bessarabia was thus unrealised.

The Russian successes in this war gave rise to apprehension in England, and in June 1790 a conference was assembled at Reichenbach under the auspices of Pitt, with a view to mediation between Russia and Turkey. Catharine, however, refused to permit any interference, and for the first time the progress of Russia formed the subject of warm debates in the House of Commons. Pitt's proposals for an increase of naval armaments, as a check to the ambitions of the Tzarina, were strongly opposed. Fox considered an alliance with Russia " the most natural and advantageous that we could possibly form." Burke stated that "the attempt to bring the Turkish Empire into consideration of the balance of Europe was extremely new, impolitic, and dangerous." He therefore protested against incurring "an immoderate expense in order to bring Christian nations under the yoke of severe and inhuman infidels." The idea of hostilities with Russia proved unpopular in the country, and the ministerial proposals were dropped and quickly forgotten on the outbreak of the war of the French Revolution.

The armies of Prussia and Austria being drawn towards the Rhine, Catharine invaded Poland in May 1792. In the following year the second partition of Poland was effected, and in 1795 the final dismemberment, by which the Baltic coast-line of Russia was extended from the head of the Gulf of Riga to its present limit, about fifteen miles north of Memel. Prussia and Spain withdrew in this year from the alliance against France; Holland was overrun by the revolutionary armies; the brunt of the war fell upon Great Britain; and Russian co-operation was at first limited to the provision of a squadron to assist in watching the Dutch ports.

The last year of the reign of the great Empress thus brought the Russian and British fleets into active alliance. On July 29th, 1795, Vice-Admiral Hanickoff, with twelve ships of the line and six frigates, joined the flag of Admiral Duncan, then entrusted with the important blockade of the Texel. During four years, with intermissions, this arrangement lasted, and its success was due to the great tact of the British admiral, which won for him the regard of his Russian subordinates. The allied squadron, however, proved deficient in sea-keeping qualities, and was generally withdrawn in the winter months. It sailed for the Baltic on June 23rd, 1797, when Admiral Duncan's force had been rendered inadequate for the duties of the blockade by the great mutiny at the Nore. It was not present at the battle of Camperdown; but two ships, the *Mistisloff* and *Ratvisan*, under Vice-Admiral Mitchell, entered the Texel on August 30th, 1799, when the Dutch fleet finally surrendered.

In November 1796, Catharine the Great died. Her land campaigns had been marked by almost unbroken success, and had advanced the boundaries of the Empire to the Niemen, the Dniester, the Black Sea, and the Sea of Azof. Peter had obtained a footing on the Baltic and built a fleet in its ports. Catharine widely extended the northern seaboard and won another in the South. The Russian navy, trained by British officers, had grown to formidable dimensions; and although in the conduct of the Swedish and the two Turkish wars no marked aptitude for naval affairs was disclosed, the experience gained was considerable. The dream of a sea-going fleet in the Euxine approached realisation, and after the Peace of Jassy ships were soon built in the southern ports. For some years, however, Turkey remained the dominant naval Power in these waters. Thus in a hundred years a semi-civilised inland people became firmly established on two seas; and while the army which Charles XII. was accustomed to defeat grew into that which nearly overcame Frederick the Great and afterwards ruined Napoleon, a new navy came into existence, and claimed at the death of

Catharine to be numerically the second in Europe. Meanwhile, during this reign the population increased from twenty-five to thirty-six millions. Unquestionably the uprising of Russia is one of the most striking developments of the eighteenth century.

During the short reign of the Tzar Paul, Russian hostility to the French Revolution at first gathered strength. A decree of January 1798, issued by the Directory, making lawful prize of neutral ships containing any article of British origin, aroused deep resentment in Russia, and in May a squadron of twenty-two ships of the line and fifty galleys was ordered to the Sound for the protection of commerce. The second coalition—Great Britain, Austria, Russia, Turkey, Naples, and Portugal—owed its existence to an opportune naval victory, and as a result of the battle of the Nile

Russian armies fought in the plains of
Northern Italy and among the mountains of Switzerland. A Russo-Turkish
squadron, in unwonted alliance, entered
the Mediterranean in September 1798,
and obtained the surrender of the Ionian
Islands ; while in May 1799 a Russian
admiral ineffectually bombarded Ancona.

Admiralty orders sent to Lord St.
Vincent in 1798 enjoined on the
Mediterranean fleet co-operation " with
the Turkish and Russian squadrons,
which are to be sent into the Archi-
pelago," and Nelson was thus brought
into contact with the youngest of
European navies. From the first he
seems to have formed an unfavourable
opinion alike of the motives and of
the efficiency of his allies. " The
Russians," he wrote to Lord Spencer
on November 29th, " seem to me to
be more bent on taking ports in the

Mediterranean than destroying Bonaparte in Egypt." On September 5th, 1799, he wrote to Captain Ball: "The Russians are anxious to get to Malta, and care for nothing else"; and to General Fox on December 14th: "The Austrians are calling out for a naval co-operation on the coast of Genoa. They complain that the Russian ships never come near them. Our Government think naturally that *eleven sail of the line, frigates, etc.*, should do something: I find they do nothing." After complaining several times of a want of co-operation, Nelson wrote to Lord Spencer on December 23rd: "The Russians, even if at sea, of which I see no prospect, cannot sail, or be of the least service. I have wrote to the Russian Minister that in my opinion the Emperor will not be well pleased with Admiral Ouschakoff."

Meanwhile, in July Sir Home Popham sailed for the Baltic to bring over a Russian contingent of seventeen thousand men, intended to co-operate in the reconquest of Holland. The Helder expedition, however, after obtaining the surrender of the Dutch fleet and some small military advantages, ended in failure. Concluding a convention with Marshal Brune, the Duke of York evacuated the country, and the Russian contingent was temporarily landed in Jersey and Guernsey.

Several causes combined to bring about the alienation of the Tzar Paul. The French projects in Egypt and in Syria, which he resented, had been thwarted by the assertion of British sea-power, and the French Mediterranean fleet had ceased to exist. Two actions, arising out of the assertion of the right of search, had been fought

between British and Danish vessels.
To want of the support of Austria
Paul attributed the disastrous retreat
of Suwarroff from Switzerland.   The
Anglo-Russian alliance in the Mediterranean had not been marked by cor-
diality, and had disclosed a divergence
of interests.   " I am persuaded," wrote
Comptroller Poussielgue from Egypt to
the Directory in 1799, "that the
English cannot see without some uneasiness, and without a secret kind of
jealousy, the progress of the Russians
—a progress much more dangerous for
them than our continental power, now
that our navy is destroyed and we
have lost our maritime conquests."

Meanwhile, Bonaparte, then First
Consul, had laboured to detach Russia
from the coalition.   In September 1800,
Malta, in which island the Tzar took a
special interest, surrendered to Great

Britain, and on December 16th the
" Armed Neutrality " was revived by
a treaty between Russia and Sweden,
to which Denmark and Prussia immediately acceded. On January 14th, Sir
Hyde Parker, with a fleet of fifty-three
sail, including eighteen ships of the line,
sailed for the Baltic. Nelson, with
the directness of purpose which was
characteristic of his genius, wished to
strike straight at the Russian squadron,
but was overruled, and the blow fell
upon Denmark. After the battle of
Copenhagen, the Swedish fleet retired
to Carlscrona and the Russians to Revel,
whither Nelson sailed the moment he
was left in command. Thence on
May 19th he wrote to Lord St. Vincent:
" On April 18th, we had eighteen sail
of the line and a fair wind. The
Russian fleet here was, I decidedly say,
at our mercy. Nothing, if it had been

right to make the attack, would have saved one ship of theirs in two hours after our entering the bay." Paul had, however, been murdered on March 24th, and the young Tzar, Alexander I., was, in Nelson's opinion, anxious for peace, provided that an arrangement could be made which did not have the appearance of compulsion. The interesting letters which passed between the British admiral and Count Pahlen support this view. The former desired to take a squadron to Revel or Cronstadt, "to mark the friendship which, I trust in God, will ever subsist between our two gracious sovereigns, and it will likewise be of great service in assisting to navigate to England many of the English vessels who have remained all the winter in Russia. I have taken care in the squadron which I bring up with me that there shall be neither bomb-ship, fire-ship, nor any of the flotilla, in order to mark the more strongly that I wish it to be considered as a mark of the greatest personal respect to his Imperial Majesty." The appearance of a British squadron in a Russian port at this juncture was evidently capable of another interpretation, and Count Pahlen firmly opposed the project. On May 18th, however, he notified the removal of the embargo on British shipping, and stated that the Tzar particularly wished to make the acquaintance of " the hero of the Nile," if he would come with a single vessel. Replying on May 26th, Nelson deferred acceptance of this invitation, adding : " I have now only to pray that a permanent (which must be honourable) peace may be established between our gracious sovereigns." On June 5th, a treaty was signed involving mutual concessions, and it is significant that, at a time when, in the words of Captain Mahan, " the British navy was superior to the combined forces of Europe," the right to trade between the ports of a belligerent was accorded to Russia.

CHAPTER V.

UNTIL 1805 Alexander took no part
in the great European war which re-
commenced on the rupture of the brief
Peace of Amiens; but in 1803 a
Russian army under Prince Zizianoff defeated the Persians near the Araxes, and
completed the subjugation of Georgia,
which had been formally annexed to
the empire in September 1801. The
speech from the throne on January
15th, 1805, indicated the approaching
conclusion of an anti-French alliance.

" I am engaged in confidential inter-
course and connexion with the Emperor
of Russia, who has given the strongest
proofs of the wise and dignified senti-
ments by which he is animated, and
of the warm interest he has taken in
the safe independence of Europe." A
treaty of offensive alliance, to which
Austria and Sweden acceded, was
signed on April 10th. By Nelson, in the
Mediterranean, the prospects of a fresh
period of Russian co-operation were
not viewed with enthusiasm. He had
previously formed a low estimate of
the efficiency of the Russian navy, and
he doubted the sincerity of the Russian
policy. "If Russia goes to war with
France," he wrote to Sir H. Elliott
on July 8th, 1804, " I hope it will be
her own war, and not joined with us.
Such alliances have never benefited
our country. . . . No ; Russia will take

care of the Ionian Republic, the Morea, and in the end Constantinople. The views of Russia are perfectly clear." Again on August 3rd he emphasised his suspicions in a letter to Sir A. J. Ball: "My opinion of the views of Russia has long been formed, and to this moment I see everything she does works to the same end—the possession of all European Turkey." Nelson's misgivings were not at this time justified. Alexander I. loyally upheld the alliance, and put one hundred and forty-six thousand men into the field. Owing mainly to the opposition of the Prussian Court to the passage of the northern army through part of Prussia, Kutusoff did not arrive in time to succour Mack at Ulm ; but Bagration made a gallant attempt to stem the advance of Murat towards Moravia, and at Austerlitz the Russian army displayed great fighting

qualities.   When Austria, concluding
the separate Treaty of Pressburg, withdrew from the coalition, Alexander
proved staunch, and at once offered to
give practical effect to the treaty of
amity which he had made with Prussia
on November 3rd.   Hesitating when
her intervention might have saved
Germany, Prussia was at length goaded
into ill-timed hostility nine months after
Austerlitz had been lost, and her collapse
after Jena left Russia face to face with
Napoleon.

Meanwhile, the defeat of Austerlitz,
followed by the defection of Austria,
wrecked the projects of the Allies.   The
King's German Legion re-embarked
for England; the Swedes retired to
Stralsund; and a combined Russo-
British expedition to Naples was withdrawn.   The Russian contingent, subsequently transported to Corfu, made a

descent upon the Dalmatian coast, and
occupied Cattaro on March 3rd, 1806.
In September, the Russian squadron
unsuccessfully blockaded Ragusa, which
was held by Lauriston.

In view of the coming campaign
against Russia, Napoleon dispatched
General Sebastiani to Constantinople.
"*Le but constant de ma policie,*" he wrote
to Talleyrand on June 9th, 1806, "*est
de faire une triple alliance de moi, de la
Porte et de la Perse, dirigée indirectement
ou implicitement contre la Russie. . . .
Le but de toutes les négociations doit être
la fermeture du Bosphore aux Russes, et
l'interdiction du passage de la Medi-
terranée à tous leurs bâtiments armés ou
non armés.*" In anticipation of Turkish
hostility, Rear-Admiral Sir Thomas
Louis was sent to the Dardanelles, and
on October 28th, 1806, the *Canopus*
anchored off Seraglio Point, where on

December 25th the Russian ambassador
was embarked. On February 19th,
1807, Sir John Duckworth, with eight
ships of the line, two frigates, and two
bomb-vessels, forced the passage of the
Dardanelles. The Russian Admiral
Seniavin, who had been brought up in
the British navy, received orders to
send four ships of the line to join
Duckworth's squadron ; but this contingent failed to arrive in time to take
part in the operation. After Duckworth's retreat, Seniavin, with eight
ships of the line, joined the British
squadron off Cape Janizarry, and is said
to have urged in vain the return of the
combined fleet to Constantinople.

During the abortive and discreditable
British expedition to Egypt, Seniavin's
squadron blockaded the Dardanelles,
while another Russian force watched
the eastern outlet of the Bosphorus.

Encouraged by Duckworth's retreat, the Turks fitted out a considerable squadron, which passed through the Dardanelles on May 19th, and was chased back by the Russians on the 22nd, with the loss of three ships by stranding. On June 22nd, the Turkish squadron again passed the Dardanelles, and troops were disembarked to occupy Tenedos. On the same day an action was fought off Lemnos, in which the Turks lost one ship captured and five driven on shore. As a result of this action, Seniavin obtained, on July 20th, the surrender of the Turkish force of four thousand six hundred men holding Tenedos.

Meanwhile, the land campaign had ended unfavourably for the Russian arms. Eylau, fought on February 7th, was barely a victory to Napoleon; but Kamenskoi's attempt to relieve

Danzig by disembarking twelve thousand men at Weichselmunde proved a failure, and the fortress surrendered to Lefebre on May 27th. Friedland followed on June 14th; and although Barclay de Tolly urged further resistance, Alexander I. concluded the Peace of Tilsit on the 25th.

The French alliance, hastily arranged on the raft in the Niemen, was from the first unpopular in Russia. It involved wars with Great Britain, Austria, and Sweden, and it lasted for less than five years amid increasing signs of estrangement.

As a result of the Peace of Tilsit, the the naval situation in the Mediterranean underwent a curious transformation. The Russian squadron, which had been acting in full concert with the British fleet, was suddenly placed in a position of quasi-belligerency, and

alarm for its safety was at once manifested. Napoleon, who less than two
years previously had issued futile in-
structions to Decrés to capture the
Russian squadron believed to be about
to enter the Mediterranean—"*Si l'on
peut les prendre, donnez ordres qu'on
ne les manque pas*"—was now gravely
concerned for his new friends. Prince
Eugene was directed to send a "brig
or a frigate" to carry the orders of
the Tzar to his admiral. A series of
letters followed, giving anxious direc-
tions that the Russian ships were to
be received and supplied in French
ports, "*pour qu'ils soient à l'abri de
toute crainte des Anglais.*" Meanwhile,
Seniavin, dispatching Rear-Admiral
Greig with two ships of the line and
some small craft to take possession of
the Ionian Islands, sailed out of the
Mediterranean with nine ships of the

line, and, entering the Tagus, was there blockaded. When the Convention of Cintra was signed on August 31st, 1808, these ships were handed over to Great Britain under a separate arrangement concluded between Admiral Seniavin and Sir Charles Cotton. The officers and crews were sent to Russia, and the ships were restored at the end of the war. The vessels left in the Mediterranean seem to have eventually fallen into the hands of the Austrians, and after the capture of Trieste in May 1809 Napoleon in a Bulletin of the Army of Germany recorded " *la délivrance de l'escadre russe* " as a circumstance "*très agréable à l'Empereur.*"

While the Russian fleet in the Mediterranean was not assailed after Tilsit, and war was not declared, a great British expedition, with seventeen ships of the line, twenty-one frigates, and

transports carrying twenty thousand
troops, descended upon Zealand, and
after bombardment Copenhagen capitu-
lated on September 7th, 1807. Seventy-
six vessels, together with large quantities of naval stores, were carried off, and
the Danish navy was obliterated.

Russia, Prussia, and Denmark now
formed a new coalition, to which
Sweden, after Admiral Gambier's fleet
had returned to England, was temporarily compelled to accede. At this
period Russia is stated to have had
twenty effective ships of the line with
fifteen hundred and eighty-eight guns,
and fourteen frigates with four hundred
and twenty-six guns, in the Baltic;
while Sweden disposed of eleven ships
of the line and six or seven frigates.
Russia was now formally at war with
Great Britain, and at the end of May
1808 Sir James Saumarez, with eleven

ships of the line, and two hundred transports conveying twelve thousand troops
under Sir John Moore, sailed for the
Baltic. This great expedition seems to
have started without any clear idea as to
what was to be attempted, and after in-
effectual negotiations with Gustavus IV.
the military force was withdrawn and
dispatched to the Peninsula.

Early in August, a Russian squadron
of twelve ships of the line with eight
frigates, under Vice-Admiral Hanickoff,
sailed from Cronstadt, arriving in Hangö
Bay on the 19th. On August 20th,
Sir Samuel Hood, with the *Centaur* and
Implacable, joined the Swedes in Oro
Sound, where on the following day the
Russians arrived. On the 22nd, the
Swedes received a reinforcement of four
ships, and the Anglo-Swedish force then
amounted to twelve sail of the line and
five frigates, of which only two vessels

were British. The Russian squadron,
which contained three 50-gun ships,
and was slightly inferior in numerical
strength, stood away for Rogerswick, and
was chased by the allied fleet. Much
straggling occurred, and the *Implacable*,
outsailing her consorts, succeeded in
bringing the *Sevolod* to action, but was
called off when the Russians bore down to
the rescue. Later the *Sevolod* was again
engaged by the *Centaur* when entering
the port, and was surrendered and
burned. On the 30th, Sir James Saumarez, with four sail of the line, joined
the force blockading Rogerswick. The
Russians were anchored close inshore, and
protected by batteries ; a boom served
to keep off fireships ; and a bombardment effected nothing. In October,
the blockading force withdrew, and
Hanickoff returned to Cronstadt. The
Sevolod had been well fought, losing

three hundred and three men ; but the Russian fleet had declined action, and in these circumstances Sir J. Saumarez, unprovided with a military force, could not obtain any definite results. The conditions were somewhat similar to those which arose nearly fifty years later. Unsupported in Finland, the Swedish cause was lost, and in November the province was ceded to the Tzar.

In 1809, several boat attacks were made in the Baltic. On the night of July 7th a Russian flotilla, lying under Porcola Point in the Gulf of Finland, was attacked by seventeen boats under Lieutenant Hawkey of the *Implacable*, who was killed. Of eight Russian gunboats only one escaped, and twelve coasting craft containing stores for the army were taken. On July 25th, three gunboats and an armed brig were suc-

cessfully cut out in Aspo Roads. Naval
operations subsequently languished;
British merchantmen seem to have found
their way into Russian ports, and this
irregular trade soon aroused the sus-
ceptibilities of Napoleon. On October
13th, 1810, he wrote to de Champagny,
directing remonstrances on the growing
violations of the " Continental System "
to be addressed to Kourakine. The
unnatural alliance patched together at
Tilsit was near the breaking-point,
and on April 8th, 1811, Napoleon wrote
to Decrés asking for information as to
the Russian and Swedish fleets in the
Baltic, and adding : " *Je viendrai à fixer
mes idées là-dessus.*" French writers
were employed to proclaim that Russia
was a menace to Europe, and Lesur
published his book containing the
apocryphal will of Peter the Great.
On June 24th, the Grand Army crossed

the Niemen, and Russia became the faithful ally of Great Britain in a great war which brought the troops of both nations to Paris in 1814 and again in 1815. The sympathy aroused in this country towards the Russian people is shown by the fact that, in addition to a Parliamentary grant, about half a million sterling was collected by private subscription for the relief of the sufferers from the burning of Moscow.

During these years the Russian arms prospered in the South. Silistria and Turtukai were taken in 1810, and Kamenskoi reconquered Bulgaria up to the Balkans. A flotilla, brought from the Black Sea, co-operated in the blockade of Rustchuk, but otherwise the operations were purely military. Peace was concluded with the Sultan in 1812, Moldavia and Wallachia being restored, and Bessarabia, together with the fortresses of Khotin and Bender, retained by Russia. Alexander I. died in 1825, after a reign which contributed largely to the expansion of the Empire. Mingrelia in 1802, and Bessarabia by the Treaty of Bucharest in 1812, were annexed, and the Treaty of Gulistan in 1814 stripped Persia of a great tract of her northern territory. Meanwhile, the Russian population rose to fifty-six millions.

In 1826, the year following the accession of the Tzar Nicholas, a new Persian war began, which ended in February 1828 by the advancement of the Russian frontier to the Araxes. The long struggle of the Greeks for independence, commencing in 1821, led at length to the Treaty of June 1827, by which France, Russia, and Great Britain agreed to take joint action in certain contingencies. Whether by accident or design, this Concert of Powers took practical shape in Navarino Bay on October 20th. The Russian squadron, under Rear-Admiral Count de Heyden, which formed the lee line, did not take a prominent part in the action, and its proceedings were not mentioned in Sir Edward Codrington's dispatch. The destruction of the Turkish fleet, however, conferred an extremely important advantage on Russia in the Turkish war which immediately followed. For the first time the Russian navy played a dominant *rôle* in the Black Sea. Kustendji in the first campaign, and Varna in the second, could consequently be made the sea bases of the Russian armies. Anapa fell to an expeditionary force dispatched from the Crimea, and Poti, captured by Paskievich, became a port of supply for the operations in Asia Minor. When peace was signed

at Adrianople in September 1829, the
success of the Russian arms was complete, and that success was largely due
to the naval command of the Black Sea
projected by Peter the Great and at
last attained. As successful was the
short Persian war which ended with
the Treaty of Turkomanchai of February 21st, 1828, and added the
provinces of Erivan and Naktchivan
to the territory of the Tzars, while
conferring on them the sole right of
maintaining ships of war on the
Caspian.

For twenty-four years Russia and
Turkey remained at peace, and Russian
naval enterprise received no direct impulse. During these years Russian
troops were employed in suppressing
the Polish insurrection of 1831 and the
Hungarian revolution of 1848. Meanwhile, in Central Asia and the Far

East, Russian projects began to assume definite shape. As early as 1822 Count Mouravieff reported to his Government that " Khiva is at this moment an advanced post which impedes our commerce with Bokhara and Northern India " ; but successive expeditions in this direction failed, and the occupation of Khiva was delayed till 1873. The Persian attacks on Herat in 1837-38, directed by Russian officers, provoked a British demonstration in the Persian Gulf, which led to the Shah's withdrawal from Afghan territory. The disaster of 1842, due mainly to military incompetence, put an end to the dream of a British advance into Central Asia, and left the way open to Russia. In 1841, the important island of Ashurada in the south-eastern corner of the Caspian was occupied; in 1847, the formation of a flotilla on the Sea of

Aral was commenced, and in 1853 two steamers were launched upon the Syr Daria. An advantageous commercial treaty between Russia and China was one of the causes of the war of 1840-41, during which Great Britain occupied, abandoned, and retook Chusan, reached Nan-king, and obtained permanent possession of Hong-kong. In the Far East, Russia displayed fresh activity, encroaching upon Chinese territory, concluding a second treaty of commerce in 1851,* and strengthening her position on the Lower Amur.

* The Treaty of Kuldja, August 25th.

CHAPTER VI.

THE CHANGE TO STEAM—THE CRIMEAN WAR—ARMOURCLADS—PRINCE GOR-TCHAKOFF'S NOTE.

DURING the long European peace which followed the settlement of 1815, the Russian fleet was well maintained. Lord Clarence Paget, who visited Cronstadt in 1839, stated that the Baltic squadron numbered " twenty-seven sail of the line, with a respectable number of frigates and small craft." He described the ships as " remarkably well found, and all that I saw peculiarly good in gun-exercise." Simple manœuvres in smooth water were " creditably " performed, " if not quite so quick as might be." Cronstadt had been made into a strong naval base, and Sebastopol, founded by Catharine II. in 1784, was after 1830 provided with docks and defences designed by an English engineer. The revolt of Mehemet Ali in 1840 led to a convention by which Russia, Austria, Prussia, and Great Britain undertook to support the Ottoman Empire. No Russian vessel, however, took part in the bombardment of Acre on November 3rd, in which three Austrian vessels and the Turkish flagship co-operated.

The change to steam propulsion had already begun, and four paddle steamers were present at Acre. Six years later the *Terrible*, of eighteen hundred and fifty tons burthen, the most formidable steam warship of the day, was commissioned, while the success of the *Archimedes*, of eighteen hundred and

forty tons, the first screw vessel of the
Royal Navy, was soon followed by the
application of Ericsson's invention to
line-of-battle ships.   This great change,
destined to revolutionise the conditions
of naval war, was naturally disadvantageous to Russia, whose industrial
development was far behind that of the
Western nations.   The outbreak of the
Crimean War brought her for the first
time into conflict with two great naval
Powers, and her fleet was totally inadequate to the occasion, even if her
geographical disadvantages had been
less marked.   No war has ever arisen
out of causes so complex or so obscure.
It is certain that the Tzar Nicholas,
at least up to February 1853, was
sincerely anxious for a full understanding with Great Britain.   The
Russian invasion of the Principalities
ended with the raising of the siege

of Silistria on June 26th, 1854, and
so far as Turkey, the protégé of the
Western Powers, was concerned, all
danger was at an end. The allied
troops, within the sound of the guns
of the old Danube fortress, had made no
attempt to aid the Turkish cause ; but
the intervention of Austria had proved
decisive, and the Concert of Europe
appeared to be solidly established.
This was the moment chosen by France
and Great Britain to enter upon an
adventure for which neither was prepared, and of the military requirements
of which both were absolutely ignorant.*

* On July 19th, 1854, Lord Raglan wrote as
follows to the Duke of Newcastle: "The fact
must not be concealed that neither the English
nor the French admirals have been able to obtain
any information on which they can rely with
respect to the army which the Russians may des-
tine for operations in the field, or of the number
of men allotted for the defence of Sebastopol;
and Marshal St. Arnaud and myself are equally

Time has stripped the amazing diplomatic proceedings of 1853-54 of their many technical fictions ; and looking back with vision undisturbed by the passions of the moment, it is difficult to resist the conclusion that Great Britain was impelled for the first time to wage direct war with Russia for reasons mainly naval. The policy of Peter the Great, long regarded with equanimity, had at length come to be viewed with real apprehension, and the prophetic insight of Poussielgue * proved to be correct. As early as 1828 Count Pozzo di Borgo had pointed out to his Government that, " although it may not be probable that we shall see an English fleet in the Black Sea, it will be prudent to

deficient in information on these all-important questions, and there would seem to be no chance of acquiring it."
* See p. 54.

make Sebastopol very secure against
attacks from the sea. If ever England
were to come to a rupture with us, this
is the point to which she could direct
her attacks, if only she believed them
possible." The assumed menace of
Sebastopol and of the fleet it harboured,
together with the tradition that the
possession of Constantinople implied the
dominion of the world, was unquestionably a principal factor in determining
the British people to engage in the
Crimean expedition.* As certainly the
popularity of the war in this country
was mainly decided by the action of
November 30th, 1853, at Sinope.
Ordinary prudence would have sug-

* "In no event," said Lord Lyndhurst in
June 1854, "except that of extreme necessity,
ought we to make peace without previously destroying the Russian fleet in the Black Sea, and
laying prostrate the fortifications by which it is
defended."

gested the withdrawal of the light
Turkish squadron of seven frigates,
three corvettes, and two small craft
from this exposed position, and ample
warning of the impending danger was
given.* The Russian attacking squadron
under Admiral Nakhimoff consisted of
six ships of the line, and in conditions
so hopelessly unequal the issue was pre-
determined; but the so-called "mas-
sacre of Sinope" was a perfectly fair act
of war, more justifiable and less de-
structive than the battle of Navarino.†
In England, however, where the facts
were not understood, the action of

---

* The Russian squadron was known to be in the
neighbourhood ten days before the action, and
the Turkish commander had pointed out that
"it may well happen that the Imperial fleet may
incur disaster."

† War was actually in progress on the lower
Danube, and the Turks had taken the Russian
fort of St. Nicholas on the eastern shore of the
Black Sea.

Russia was regarded as a national affront especially affecting British naval prestige, and the invasion of the Crimea, with the obliteration of the Russian Black Sea squadron and its base, became a popular object. The motives which induced France to assume the leading *rôle* in the proceedings which directly tended to war are much less clear. Even if Mr. Kinglake is incorrect in attributing these proceedings entirely to the personal aims of Louis Napoleon, it is certain that there was no solidarity of interests between the Allies. With the French people the war was never widely popular, and the Emperor showed much eagerness to bring it to a close as soon as the requirements of military prestige were satisfied by the fall of Sebastopol. By a fortuitous combination of circumstances, therefore, rather than in obedience to natural laws, the two great hereditary naval and commercial rivals of the West found themselves in active alliance against a Power which on account of geographical and other conditions could be the naval rival of neither.

To Russia the war necessarily involved naval humiliation. She was not only numerically overmatched, but her fleet was far behind those of her antagonists, and that of Great Britain especially, in the application of steam propulsion. In the Black Sea, the Baltic, the White Sea, and the Sea of Okhotsk, the Allies assumed the offensive, and the Russian ships sought the shelter of their ports. The Black Sea squadron consisted of fifteen sailing ships of the line, with several frigates and brigs, one powerful steamer, the *Vladimir*, and eleven small steamers.

One chance only presented itself to the Russian commander. From September 5th, when the French put to sea, to the 18th, when the landing in the Crimea was completed, the expeditionary force of the Allies was exposed to grave risks.

The fleets, with their transports, numbered nearly two hundred vessels, and the French and Turkish warships were so crowded with troops as to be practically *hors de combat*. Order could not be rigidly preserved in such a promiscuous assemblage of steamers and sailing craft. Bad weather alone would probably have wrecked the operation. The duty of providing protection to the whole expedition was undertaken by the British force under Vice-Admiral Dundas, consisting of ten line-of-battle ships (including two provided with screws), two 50-gun frigates,

and thirteen smaller steamers heavily
armed.   The effect of an attack directed
against the non-combatant portion of
the convoy cannot be estimated.   The
force at the disposal of the British
admiral could doubtless have defeated
the Russian squadron in a fleet action ;
but, constituted as it was, it could
hardly have prevented damage to the
convoy sufficient to have frustrated the
invasion of the Crimea.   In the circumstances the attempt ought certainly
to have been made.*   The Russian
squadron, however, remained in harbour,
and on September 13th, when two line-
of-battle ships, with the smoke of a
great fleet behind them, could be made
out from Sebastopol, the wind was

* In the present days of fast steamships, it is
difficult to see how superior naval force could
protect a great fleet of transports against a determined attack in open waters.

unfavourable for proceeding to sea.
On the 21st, after the battle of the
Alma had been lost, Admiral Korniloff
assembled his officers and proposed
to attack the allied fleets. Prince
Mentschikoff had, however, already
determined to risk nothing at sea, and
the one great opportunity had passed.
On the night of the 22nd, the sinking
of the Russian ships at the entrance
of the harbour began, and Korniloff
devoted all the resources at his command to the land defence of Sebastopol.
Robbed of their proper *rôle*, the Russian
seamen played a gallant and an extremely important part in creating and
holding the improvised fortifications,
which withstood all the efforts of the
Allies till September 8th, 1855.

In the Baltic, as in the Black Sea,
the Russian navy attempted nothing.
The conditions were manifestly un-

equal; but a purely defensive attitude is peculiarly unsuited to a naval force, and there were occasions when greater enterprise might have been shown. At the outset of the war Russia had " twenty-five sail of the line which had been with their crews training in the Baltic for years," * together with a number of heavy frigates and small craft. The Allies possessed the great advantage of steam, and Sir Charles Napier's fleet in 1854 had thirteen screw line-of-battle ships; but of " sixteen sail of the line five or six were at first scarcely fit to go into action " † on account of the want of training of the crews. There seems, at the outset, to have been an impression in the

* Evidence of Admiral Sir B. J. Sulivan before the Royal Commission on Manning the Navy in 1858.

† *Ibid.*

British squadron that the Russians would show some activity; but their ships remained during 1854 under the protection of the batteries of Sveaborg and Cronstadt. The handling of the allied fleet was characterised by a conspicuous want of vigour and purpose; but it is questionable whether more could have been effected with the available resources. Bomarsund fell on August 16th to a combined attack, the land operations being, as usual in such cases, the decisive factor. Much destruction of coasting trade was carried out, which could have little or no result as regarded the main issues of the war. Cronstadt was reconnoitred and reported to contain seventeen sail of the line, and five frigates ready for sea, together with fifteen heavy gunboats. At the end of the short northern summer the sailing ships of the Allies were sent home, and plans for attacking Cronstadt were discussed and subsequently abandoned.

The only achievement of 1855 was the bombardment and destruction of the arsenal and town of Sveaborg in August, the defences remaining nearly intact. A fresh reconnaissance of Cronstadt showed only five ships of the line with sails bent. The rest were apparently moored for use as blockships, the Russians having abandoned all idea of sending a squadron to sea. Meanwhile, however, great efforts had been made for the local floating defence of the fortress, with a view to meet an attack by gun- and mortar-boats. " Twenty-three fine screw gunboats, larger, I think, than ours; some with three heavy guns each, and with a range equal to that of the heaviest guns we have," * had been prepared. These gunboats

* Letter from Admiral Sir B. J. Sulivan.

were engined from locomotive works, managed chiefly by foreigners; and their construction, in spite of the poverty of resources, is evidence of the vigour and capacity of the Russian authorities. In 1855, preparations were made in this country for attacking Cronstadt in the following year, but peace supervened. It is probable that this Baltic stronghold could have been taken in 1854, if a suitable flotilla and a large landing force had been then available. The operations in northern waters were, however, begun by the Allies with as little knowledge of the conditions there as in the Crimea, and utterly unwarranted expectations of the performance of Sir Charles Napier's fleet were forthcoming in this country. Nevertheless, it must not be assumed that those operations were fruitless. In addition to the loss due to the blockade

and the destruction effected at Bomarsund, Sveaborg, and other places, the
menace to the Baltic coast-line sufficed
for some time to detain a large number
of Russian troops in the northern provinces, and thus to indirectly aid the
siege of Sebastopol. Whether this
detention was wholly justified, in view
of the marked want of enterprise shown
by the British naval commanders, is
another matter. The Russians could
not have foretold the extreme nervous-
ness which Sir Charles Napier showed,
or the reluctance of his successor to
take the active measures against Sveaborg which were carried out without
loss.

In the White Sea and the Far East
the operations of the Allies were of
little importance; but at Petropaulovski,
on the East coast of Kamtschatka, a
reverse occurred on August 30th, 1854,

when a landing party of seven hundred men was repulsed with heavy loss. The port was again visited in May 1855, and found deserted; the fortifications were destroyed, but the Russian ships escaped.

The war, though waged mainly by military force, turned absolutely on sea-power, in which Russia was not only overmatched, but placed at great geographical disadvantage, accentuated by the want of good internal communication, which entailed heavy losses on her troops and enabled the Allies to be ultimately superior at the decisive point. In Great Britain the principal lesson was little understood till recent years. In the later policy of Russia the results of that lesson can certainly be traced.

The Allies may be said to have attained their apparent objects. For twenty-two years Russia and Turkey remained at peace, and the Eastern Question slumbered. Russian naval activity was for a time crippled, and diplomatists were able to believe that by a paper treaty indefinite restrictions could be imposed upon the actions of a great empire in its own territorial waters.

With the war of 1854-55 the era of the wooden ship and the smooth-bore gun practically ended. The success of the armourclad floating batteries employed by the French at Kinburn in October 1855 led to the conversion of the *Napoleon* into *La Gloire* in 1859, and Great Britain followed in 1861 with the *Warrior*, built entirely in iron.* The American War, and the

* This was an extremely important departure, considering that the Admiralty had previously discouraged iron construction, which had been pressed upon it as early as 1834, and was already firmly established in the mercantile marine.

memorable action of the *Monitor* and *Merrimac* in Hampton Roads, gave a fresh turn to the design of warships, which by a chequered process of evolution has led to the 14,900-ton steel battle-ships of the present day.

This vital change, which conferred immediate potential advantage upon Great Britain,* entailed great difficulties in Russia. Some wooden screw vessels were built after the Crimean War, and the *Sebastopol* and *Petropaulovski* were converted into armourclad frigates. Ten monitors were ordered in 1863, when Western intervention on behalf of Poland seemed probable. Between

---

* In the design and speed of construction of the wooden ship France had for many years a distinct advantage over this country. The change to iron, and subsequently to steel, reversed this condition, and our neighbours have not at present proved able to rival British shipbuilders either in design or in speed and economy of construction.

1860 and 1875 five sea-going armour-clads, the largest being the *Peter the Great*, of 8,750 tons, and twenty armoured coast-defence vessels, ranging from the *Admiral Spiridoff*, of 3,740 tons, to the *Ooragan*, of 1,410 tons, were launched for the Baltic fleet. During the same period the *Novgorod*, of 2,700 tons, and the *Admiral Popoff*, of 3,590 tons, were launched at Nicolaieff for the Black Sea squadron. The reconstruction of the Russian fleet thus for a time proceeded slowly, and coast-defence craft predominated.

On October 29th, 1870, when Germany and France were in the throes of a great conflict, Prince Gortchakoff's note demanding the abrogation of Clause II. of the Treaty of Paris was presented to Europe. The Black Sea Conference was assembled, and, as a result of the deliberations concluded on

March 13th, 1871, all restrictions on
Russian naval activity in the Black Sea
were formally removed. In this country
the repudiation of the famous clause
was widely regarded as a gross breach
of faith, and a blow delivered against
the sanctity of all treaties. Russia,
said Lord Stratheden and Campbell in
the House of Lords, has " openly proclaimed defiance of international engagements."   The philosophic historian of
the future will probably adopt other
views, and will deride the idea of the
professional diplomatist that a great
nation could be expected to indefinitely
acquiesce in the artificial restrictions
sought to be imposed by the Treaty
of Paris. Russia was not conquered
in 1854-55, had during a century
and a half made enormous sacrifices
in order to secure freedom of action
in the Black Sea, and was justified in

reasserting that freedom as soon as she felt ready to accept the risk of war.* The whole British nation, in similar circumstances, would have loudly demanded similar action.

* Even if France had not been fettered in 1870, it is more than doubtful whether all or any of the co-signatories of the Treaty of Paris—France, Austria, and Great Britain—would have taken up arms in defence of Clause II.

CHAPTER VII.

RUSSO-TURKISH WAR OF 1877-78—CON-
GRESS OF BERLIN — SKOBELEFF'S
· SCHEME—CREATION OF THE MODERN
FLEET.

VON MOLTKE, in his memorable study
of the war of 1828-29, foretold that, in
the next Russo-Turkish conflict, Russian
naval supremacy in the Black Sea would
be strongly asserted. This prophecy was
not fulfilled. Whether taught by history
or inspired by caprice, the Sultan Abdul
Aziz conceived the idea of creating an
armourclad fleet, and between the years
1864 and 1875 fifteen armoured ships,
ranging from the *Mesoodiyeh*, of 8,990
tons, to the *Idjlaliyeh*, of 2,240 tons, and

three gunboats of 400 to 330 tons, were launched for the Turkish Government.* When war was declared in April 1877, the Russians had no naval force with which to oppose the fleet of Abdul Aziz, and the Turkish command of the Black Sea was practically as complete as that asserted by the Allies in 1854-55.† The difficulties of the campaign were thus materially enhanced, and the invading army was compelled to force the passage of the Danube and the Balkans, and to depend for the whole

* Two of these vessels were built at Constantinople, all the rest in Great Britain or France. In addition, the Turkish Navy List of 1876 included five steam frigates, eleven corvettes, and some river gunboats. The nominal total *personnel* of the navy exceeded eighteen thousand men.

† The total of the armoured ships of Russia in 1876 is given by Lord Brassey as twenty-nine, including fourteen coast-defence monitors. Only two sea-going vessels carrying more than seven inches of armour were then completed.

of its supplies upon a lengthening line
of difficult land communications. Russian
naval activity was limited to unimportant raids on coasting craft and some
torpedo-boat work,* of which the only
result was the sinking of the Turkish
gunboat *Seifé* in the Matchin channel
of the Danube. On the other hand,
the Turks made no use of their command of the sea for offensive purposes,
and the handling of their gunboats on
the Danube at the beginning of the
campaign showed a total lack of vigour,
by which many opportunities were lost.
Thus the war took the form of two
mutually independent land campaigns
in Europe and Asia respectively; and
although the Russians suffered severely
for want of the sea-power which materially contributed to their success in the

* In the Danube the Russians had only small
steam-launches.

campaigns of 1828-29, there were certain
mitigations of their difficulties. In the
European theatre of war, road communications north and to a less extent
south of the Danube had greatly im-
proved, and railways facilitated the
primary concentration of the invading
army. In the Asiatic campaign, the
complete subjugation of Georgia and
the Caucasus, and the advance of the
frontier to Alexandropol, accomplished
after the Crimean War, proved a great
advantage. Moreover, a railway leading
to Vladikavkas, one hundred miles from
Tiflis, which had already become a
great military centre, rendered the loss
of sea communications far less serious
than in 1854-55.

In this country there was a wide-
spread belief, fostered by the negative
successes at Plevna, that the Turkish
resistance would prove effective and

prolonged. The rapid advance of
Skobeleff on Adrianople in January
1878 shattered this belief and gave rise
to uneasiness. On the 28th, the Chancellor of the Exchequer (Sir Stafford
Northcote) moved for a vote of
£6,000,000 for measures of preparation, and at the same time announced
the proposed terms of peace which had
been communicated by Count Schou-
valoff. On the night of the 31st, an
armistice was concluded which gave
the Russians possession of the lines of
Boyuk-Tchekmedji, and on February
13th the British fleet passed the Dardanelles, the Russians replying by a prompt
advance to San Stefano, six miles from
Constantinople, where peace was signed
on March 3rd.

Judged by the standard supplied to
Europe by Germany at the end of
January 1871, the terms which were

offered to Turkey appear excessively moderate ; but strong antagonism to the Russian proposals was manifested in Great Britain, and after a period during which war hung in the balance, the Treaty of San Stefano was referred to a European Congress assembled at Berlin. The naval weakness of Russia, which had hampered the operations of the campaign, rendered the position of the army before Constantinople insecure, and without any effective ally in Europe she was naturally unwilling to force an issue.

Whether Great Britain or Turkey gained any substantial advantage by the Treaty of Berlin may fairly be doubted. Speaking on January 28th, 1878, Sir Stafford Northcote's principal charge against the original Russian proposals was that "they would completely separate Constantinople and the

Balkan territory from the European possessions of Turkey." The division of Bulgaria into two portions and a stipulation that Turkey should have the right to garrison the Balkan passes were, therefore, the principal achievements of the Congress of Berlin. Bulgaria and Roumelia were united seven years later, and during those years no Turkish soldier ever set his foot on the Balkans. On the other hand, Lord Beaconsfield laid special stress on the fact that the Treaty of San Stefano would render the Black Sea a Russian lake, as has long been the case. Great Britain obtained Cyprus, which could add no strength to the Empire, giving in exchange a separate undertaking to defend the Asiatic frontier of Turkey in certain contingencies, and Austria gained in Bosnia and Herzegovina possessions of some value.

To Russia the net result of the Congress of Berlin was a diplomatic rebuff entailing no practical disadvantage. Bessarabia was added to her European possessions, and the Asiatic frontier was advanced so as to include Kars and the port of Batoum. It was provided that the latter should remain open and unfortified, but within a few years this provision was set aside.* The principal political effect of the proceedings of 1878 was to embitter Anglo-Russian relations by creating mutual

* This was a period of secret understandings, and there is reason to believe that liberty to fortify Batoum was privately conceded, although this proceeding has since been a popular ground for accusations of bad faith against Russia. Meanwhile, the result of the Russian occupation of this port has been to immensely increase the British tonnage annually entering and clearing. The figures lately given by Mr. W. S. Caine are: 1881, 14 ships, with 16,000 tonnage ; 1896, 308 ships, with 544,000 tonnage. For 1893 the figures are 529 and 806,000, so that there has been a recent decline.

suspicions, while at the same time Great Britain gained no increase of influence at Constantinople. It naturally followed that measures would be taken to promote difficulties on the Indian frontier, and at the end of May General Stolietoff left Tashkent on a mission to Kabul, which led to the Afghan War, entailing an expenditure of twenty-two millions sterling upon the people of India. Meanwhile, Skobeleff, the hero of the Turkish War, formulated a visionary scheme of invasion by organised " hordes of Asiatic horsemen, who, to a cry of blood and plunder, might be launched against India as the vanguard, thus reviving the days of Timur." This project had no military value, since "the days of Timur" happily cannot be revived, and large masses of cavalry could not subsist among the wild mountains of the frontier which Skobeleff never saw; but the existence of such impracticable schemes has exercised a powerful influence upon Indian polity.*

The lessons of the war of 1877-78 were taken to heart in Russia. Many reforms were introduced into the army, and steps were taken to increase the navy, and especially to create a Black Sea squadron. With the year 1882, a fresh period of naval development

---

* It is interesting to note that Skobeleff himself seems to have recognised that his plan involved something of the nature of a forlorn hope. "I do think," he wrote, "and we must not shut our eyes to the fact, that the undertaking would indeed be a risky one. . . . We should expect from the troops who were so fortunate as to be selected for this campaign something more than self-sacrifice in its highest sense. . . . On crossing the Hindu-Kush, the column should, in my opinion, be so handled that every man might feel that he had come to conquer or to die—that each man might understand that the Tzar required even his death."

began.   In 1886, the *Tchesmé* and the
Catharine II., and in 1887 the *Sinope*
(Fig. 1), battle-ships of 10,180 tons,
were launched, forming the nucleus of
the present powerful Black Sea fleet.
At the same time the construction of
a large torpedo-boat flotilla was commenced.   Naval progress has since
steadily proceeded, and in 1896
the following vessels were built or
building * :—

CLASS.	No.	TONS.
Battle-ships	19	179,000
Armoured cruisers	11	82,273
Coast-defence armourclads ...	16	48,738
Protected cruisers	5	25,038
Unprotected cruisers	3	8,400
Torpedo gun-vessels	17	13,776
Destroyers	5	—
Torpedo-boats over 100 feet ...	74	—

* Taken from an Admiralty Return of August
1896.

The corresponding figures for the present year are * :—

CLASS.	No.	TONS.
Battle-ships	20	215,341
Armoured cruisers	11	82,223
Coast-defence armourclads ...	22	60,300
Protected cruisers	9	51,571
Unprotected cruisers (3rd class)	20	32,519
Torpedo gun-vessels	9	4,270
Destroyers	5	1,200
Torpedo-boats over 100 feet ...	75	—

In addition there are twenty-seven auxiliary cruisers, of which thirteen, forming the so-called "Volunteer Fleet," are always prepared to receive an armament in war.

The Black Sea squadron now numbers seven battle-ships † (exclusive of three building), seven cruisers, and nine

* *The Naval Pocket Book*, 1898.
† *Sinope* (Fig. 1), *Catharine II.*, *Tchesmé* (10,180 tons); *Dvienadyat Apostoloff* (8,700 tons); *Georgi Podbiedonosetz* (10,280 tons); *Tria Sviatitelia* (12,480 tons) (Fig. 6); *Rostilaf* (8,800 tons).

auxiliaries, together with armoured coast-defence craft and a strong torpedo-boat flotilla. The *personnel* numbers about 11,600 men of all ranks.

The Baltic squadron numbers eight battle-ships * (exclusive of two nearly ready for launching), with cruisers, coast-defence vessels, and a torpedo-boat flotilla. The *personnel* numbers about 28,900 officers and men.

The official classification given by Lieut. A. Stroumillo in the *Naval Annual* for 1898 is as follows :—

> *First rate:* Imperial yachts, battle-ships, coast-defence ironclads, first-class cruisers ; total, 45 vessels.
>
> *Second rate:* Coast-defiance ironclads of smaller

---

* *Poltava, Petropaulovsk, Sebastopol* (10,950 tons); *Alexander II.* (9,930 tons); *Nicolai I.* (9,670 tons); *Navarin* (10,200 tons); *Sissoi Veliky* (8,800 tons) (Fig. 5) ; and *Peter Veliky* (4,890 tons). The *Peresviet* and *Osliabia* (12,475 tons) are to be launched this year.

dimensions, sea-going gunboats, training-ships, second-class cruisers, torpedo-cruisers, steamers, transports ; total, 67 vessels.

Third rate : Coast-defence gunboats, sea-going torpedo-boats, coastguard-ships, light-ships ; total, 145 vessels.

Fourth rate : Small torpedo-craft and other small vessels ; total, 125 vessels.

The ships now building or completing are * :—

First-class battle-ships	6
Second-class battle-ship	1
Coast-defence armourclad	1
Armoured cruiser	1
Protected cruisers	4
Destroyers	17
Gunboats	3

The latest programme contemplates laying down three battle-ships of 12,675 tons on the Neva this summer, and three more as soon as building-slips become available. In addition, one

* *Times*, May 4th.

battle-ship and one cruiser will be ordered from Messrs. Cramp of Phila-
delphia, and fifteen or twenty destroyers
will also be put out to foreign contract.*

During the five years 1880-84, the
expenditure on the Russian navy increased from £3,140,000 to £3,730,000,
and amounted in all to £16,445,700.
Between 1890 and 1897 the growth was
as follows † :—

YEAR.				£
1890	...	...	...	... 4,311,350
1891	...	...	...	... 4,813,600
1892	...	...	...	... 5,267,000
1893	...	...	...	... 5,488,250
1894	...	...	...	... 5,635,400
1895	...	...	...	... 6,042,650
1896	...	...	...	... 6,376,250
1897	...	...	...	... 6,589,250
1898	...	...	...	... 7,000,000

The special appropriation for new

* *Times*, May 4th and 14th.
† These figures are taken from *Die Ausgaben
für Flotte und Landheer*, compiled by the German
Admiralty, 1898.

construction to be spread over the next seven years amounts to nearly £20,000,000. The total *personnel* now actively employed afloat and ashore numbers about 44,000 men.

The above figures imply a remarkable development. Russia, as a naval power, now stands third among the great States of the world ; and although, judged by the number of her ships, she stood second at the end of the reign of Catharine II., the creation of the modern fleet since the Turkish war of 1877-78 must be regarded as an achievement unparalleled in her history. All the sea-going war-ships of this fleet have been built in Russia, and foreign assistance, freely sought at first, is every year becoming less necessary.* In gun con-

* All the ships of the so-called Volunteer Fleet, as well as many vessels employed on the Caspian and the Siberian rivers, were built in Great Britain.

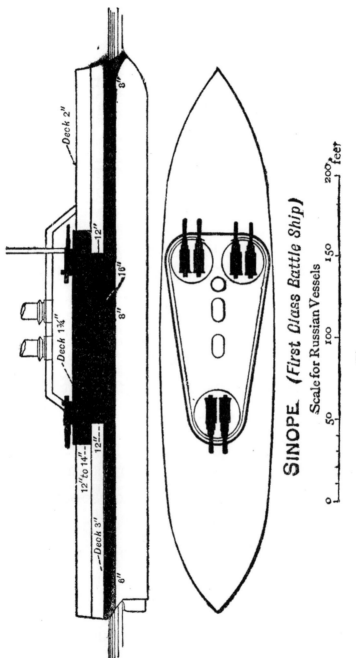

SINOPE. (First Class Battle Ship)

Scale for Russian Vessels

Fig. I.

Deck 2"

12"

16"

8"

Deck 1¾"

8"

12" to 14"

12"

Deck 3"

6"

8"

50   100   150   200 feet

struction the advance has been equally marked. The great works at Abuhoff on the Neva, under the Ministry of Marine, can now make excellent ordnance of all sizes, and the latest 12-inch gun of nearly 56 tons is fully equal to any weapon of similar calibre elsewhere produced.

Considering the general backwardness of Russia in industrial science only twenty-five years ago, the rapid growth of the modern fleet is a most significant sign of national progress. Russia has accomplished a task which might have been deemed impossible.

In design, the Russian Ministry of Marine has shown both originality and initiative. The pear-shaped redoubts of the three battle-ships of the *Sinope* class (see Fig. 1), enabling six heavy guns to be mounted in pairs, are peculiar to the Russian navy. No battle-ship of 13,000 tons has yet been built, and the

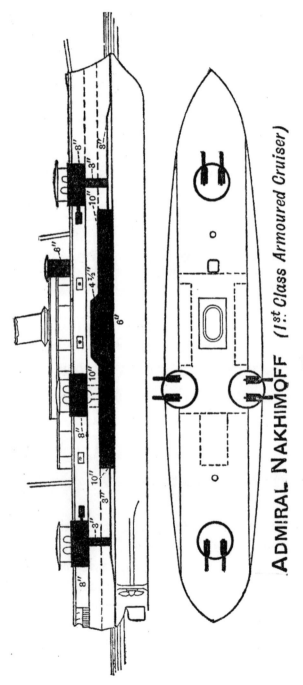

ADMIRAL NAKHIMOFF (1st Class Armoured Cruiser)

Fig. 2.

temporary craze for monster guns which we borrowed from Italy * never reached Russia, where the 12-inch gun is the largest afloat.

The armoured cruiser *Nakhimoff* (Fig. 2), of 7,780 tons, launched in 1885, is peculiar in her powerful armament of eight 8-inch guns placed in pairs in armoured barbettes.

In the *Rurik* † (see Fig. 4), of 10,940 tons and 18 knots speed, launched in 1894, a lead was given to the navies of the world in the construction of large armoured cruisers. The *Rossia*, of 12,130 tons and 20 knots, was launched in 1896 ‡ ; and the *Gromoboy*, of 14,000

---

* This craze inflicted upon the British navy the *Sanspareil* and *Victoria*, which must be reckoned among the worst armourclads ever built.

† Developed from the *Pamyat Azova* (Fig. 3), launched at St. Petersburg in 1888.

‡ The *Rossia* was present at Spithead at the Jubilee review of 1897.

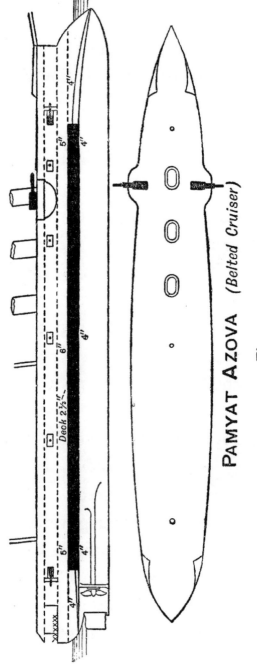

PAMYAT AZOVA *(Belted Cruiser)*

Fig. 3.

tons, was laid down in 1897. The effect of the appearance of the *Rurik* was quickly seen in the launch of our *Powerful* and *Terrible*, of 14,200 tons and 21 knots (nominal), launched in 1895, and in the *Diadem* class, of 11,000 tons and 20·5 knots, of which the first vessel was launched in 1896. The design of the great Russian cruisers is open to criticism, but they unquestionably marked a new departure by surpassing in tonnage and speed our *Blake* and *Blenheim*, launched in 1889 and 1891 respectively. The later Russian battle-ships, such as the *Tria Sviatitelia* (see Fig. 6), conform nearly to our *Canopus* type, but are more heavily armoured.

The relative fighting value of navies is generally more difficult to determine than that of armies. The elements of strength of different ships are matters of dispute. War is the only real test of

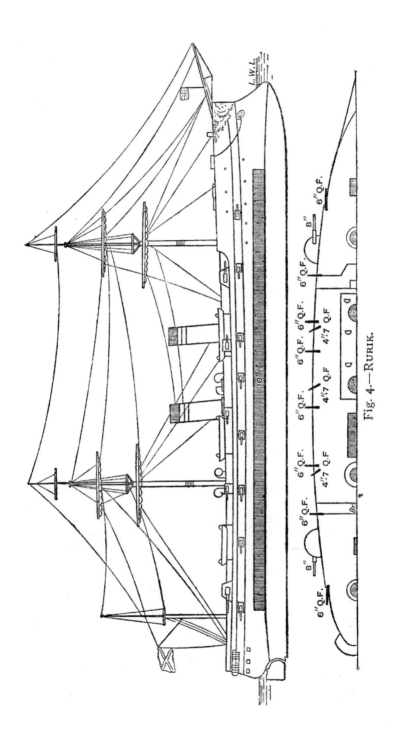

L.W.L.

6" Q.F.   6" Q.F.   B"   6" Q.F.   6" Q.F.   6" Q.F.   4".7 Q.F.   4".7 Q.F.   6" Q.F.   6" Q.F.   4".7 Q.F   6" Q.F.   6" Q.F.   B"   6" Q.F.

Br.

Fig. 4.—RURIK.

their efficiency, and rough usage of their seaworthiness, and of the competence of their technical staffs. There is evidence that grave structural defects have appeared in vessels built in Russian dockyards,* and administrative scandals have occurred. Russian naval prestige, as has been shown, rests wholly upon her wars with Sweden and Turkey in the last century. If the ambitions of Charles XII. had taken a naval rather than a military shape, the far wiser aspirations of Peter the Great would have been less quickly realised. It was a Sweden in her decadence that Russia successfully opposed at sea, and the seamen by whom Russian victories were won were largely drawn from the population of Swedish provinces. Moreover, the

---

* The loss of the *Gangut* off Viborg on June 24th, 1897, has been attributed to such defects.

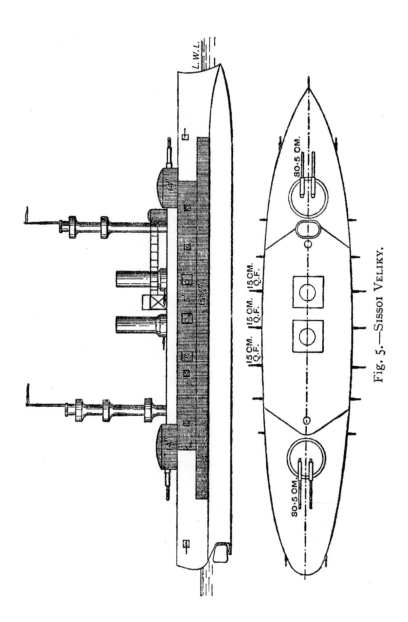

Fig. 5.—Sissoi Veliky.

Russian navy of the eighteenth century owed its fighting efficiency mainly to British officers. The Turks were never a great naval nation, and the fighting in the Black Sea resolved itself principally into affairs of flotillas, while the victory of Tchesmé was wholly due to the skill and gallantry of Scotchmen. At Navarino no serious demand was made upon the Russian squadron, and at Sinope the conditions were so unequal as to preclude deductions. In the past the Russian navy has not shown marked enterprise, produced great naval commanders, or proved conspicuous in seamanlike ability. Nelson's aphorism, "Close with a Frenchman and out-manœuvre a Russian," expressively sums up the opinion of the greatest of admirals. Ancient traditions and inherited aptitudes are wanting to the Russian Empire, which has been built

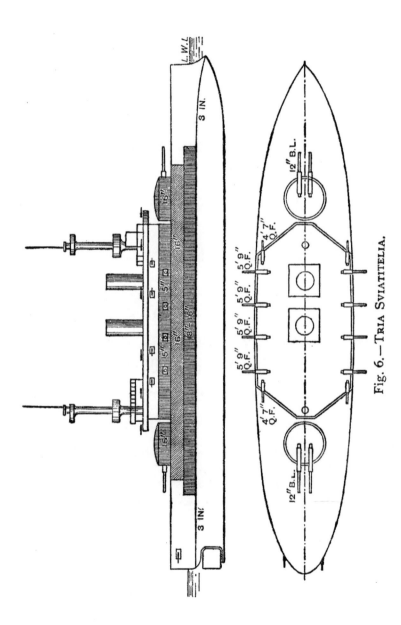

Fig. 6.—Tria Sviatitelia.

up from an inland centre by a people who with set purpose extended their dominion outwards to the sea. Sea-borne commerce, which has been alike the support and the educating force of other nations, has played little or no part in the development of Russia.

The total value of the sea-borne commerce of the Russian Empire is stated in an Admiralty Return of 1895 to be £69,665,220, including bullion and specie, and excluding all except " imports for home consumption and exports of domestic produce." The aggregate tonnage of the mercantile marine is given as 487,681 in the same Return, only vessels of 100 tons gross and upwards being included.

Even now, therefore, the maritime interests of Russia are small relatively to those of Great Britain, the United States,

and Germany.*   Russia is a naval but
not a great maritime State, and is consequently deprived of one of the prime
elements of sea-power.   Unique geographical disabilities and a tardy evolution sufficiently explain the fact that
the Russian navy is an artificial rather
than a national product.

On the other hand, the great fighting
qualities of the Russian people have
been abundantly attested, and Nelson's
words imply a well-deserved tribute to
their powers of stubborn endurance.
Now and for many years to come
poverty of technical resources and the
low standard of intelligence of the
Russian conscript sailor † must militate

* Spain in the same Return shows an aggregate
sea-borne trade of £55,105,000, and a mercantile
tonnage of 554,238.

† The contrast in the appearance of the Russian
sailors and British, or French Breton and Norman
bluejackets, is most striking, and the results of
education in quickening the intelligence are evident.

against naval efficiency; but the great fleet built and building must nevertheless be regarded as a formidable force. Only the test of war can show whether the Russian people have been fully able, in the words of Peter the Great, " to conquer the art of the sea."

Politically the effects of the naval renaissance of Russia have already been significantly manifested. The fact that navies are powerful agents for the interchange of national sentiment is little recognised, although the influence of the presence of British squadrons in the ports of our great colonies is one of the principal factors in promoting and maintaining the unity of the Empire. Out of the visits of Russian and French squadrons to each other's ports sprang an alliance which has already borne fruits of importance. The Russian and French people know nothing of each other, and are unlike in most essential respects. The visits of the respective squadrons touched the imagination of the masses as no diplomatic correspondence could have done. It was something which those masses could understand. Throughout the complicated performances of the so-called " Concert of Europe," the strong position asserted by Russia was due mainly to her powerful " fleet in being " in the Black Sea. Turkey, for whose sake we made immense sacrifices in 1854-55, and on whose behalf we were nearly led into making even greater sacrifices in 1878, is now almost the vassal of Russia; and the strategists, who found occupation in planning great campaigns in which Turkish armies, led by British officers, were to perform military prodigies in the Caucasus, have of late preserved a significant silence. The great stride in the Far East which

has carried Russia from the banks of
the Amur to the Gulf of Pe-chi-li was
brought within the scope of practical
politics by the creation of the fleet.
The policy is precisely that of Peter the
Great; only the method differs somewhat
with the changed circumstances of the
times. It was necessary for Peter from
his inland State to conquer a seaboard
on the Baltic and the Euxine, and when
there established to build up a navy.
Vladivostock, the Russian station in the
Far East, has for years been supported
from the sea ; and when the German
descent upon the province of Shan-tung
was accomplished, and the practical dismemberment of China began, it was the
possession of a powerful fleet which
enabled the advisers of the Tzar to
ante-date their plans by the occupation
of Ta-lien-wan and Port Arthur. In
1702-3, Peter's troops overran Ingria

and Livonia, and captured Nöteburg
and Nyen, enabling a fleet to be built
in the Gulf of Finland.   In 1898, the
navy of Nicholas II., built in Europe,
establishes itself in the ports of the Liao-
tong Peninsula, and land forces are prepared to move to the support of the
navy.

CHAPTER VIII.

RUSSIAN EXPANSION——LINES OF ADVANCE — THE FAR EAST — THE LATEST STEP — THE RUSSIAN NAVAL POSI-TION.

From the naval point of view, the crucial phases in the expansion of Russia were those which gave her a seaboard and harbours in the Baltic, the Black Sea, and the Far East. The first was accomplished by Peter the Great, and the Baltic fleet which he inaugurated has never suffered a great reverse, although it was effectually neutralised and confined to its ports by the superior force of the Allies in 1854-55. The second was achieved by Catharine II. ;

but the Russian command of the Black
Sea was not actually asserted till the
Turkish war of 1827-28, and twenty-
seven years later Russian sea-power in
these waters was shattered by the
Crimean War, not to be fully restored
until the great naval movement of 1882
began to take effect. The third has
just received a fresh development of the
most important character.

For nearly two hundred years the
policy of obtaining, maintaining, and
increasing a seaboard has been con-
sistently followed. If that policy was
inaugurated by Peter the Great, it was
nevertheless absolutely due to the operation of irresistible natural forces. A
great nation must seek a seaboard corresponding in extent to its needs, and
Russia could no more be restrained in
her seaward expansion than could the
United States in overflowing the Rocky

Mountains in their march to the Pacific. The policy thus forced upon Russia by the conditions of her being has involved many wars and great sacrifices. The methods adopted have been various, and, in common with those which have commended themselves to all nations, have not been wholly blameless; but only the curious inability of the British people to realise the necessities of others can blind us to the fact that Russian expansion was as inevitable as our own. To the fifty millions of Great and Greater Britain free access to the sea is the breath of national life; by the eighty millions of Russia the same vital need is instinctively felt.

A glance at the map serves to show that, after nearly two centuries of effort, the conditions of Russia, from the maritime point of view, remain exceptionally disadvantageous. The British

Empire has free access to all the oceans
and seas of the world. France faces
the Atlantic and holds fourteen hundred
miles of the shores of the Mediterranean.
Spain is admirably placed for the
exercise of sea-power. Germany, by
means of the North Sea Canal, holds an
outlet to blue water in her own hands.
The United States front two oceans.
Japan is almost as favourably situated
as the British Islands. Russia, on the
other hand, by a freak of circumstance,
unfortunate for herself and other nations,
has her sea-communications in Europe
land-locked and partially ice-locked, and
the effect of these great geographical
disadvantages was manifested in the
Crimean War. In the Far East,
Kamtschatka, annexed in 1697, has its
spring, summer, and autumn compressed
into four months. Vladivostock, which
became a Russian port in 1860, is

ice-locked for about four months,* and
is situated in the almost inland Sea of
Japan. Even Port Arthur, the latest
acquisition, does not provide such un-
impeded access to the ocean as is given
by Brest, Cadiz, New York, or San
Francisco, and has the additional draw-
back of being fully four thousand four
hundred miles by the shortest railway
route from the Russian capital. A
further possible outlet exists in the
Persian Gulf, recommended in M.
Lesur's version of the will of Peter
the Great ; but here also the conditions
are evidently unfavourable, since access
to the Indian Ocean is throttled by the
Straits of Ormuz.†

* Efforts have for some time been made to
keep Vladivostock open in winter by means of
steam ice-breakers.

† Attention has at various times been drawn
to another possible outlet. Some years ago a
concession was obtained by a British company

The purely territorial expansion of
Russia, arrested in the West since 1814
by Prussia (now Germany) and Austria,
and hampered in the South-west by
the various international interests which
from time to time have rallied to pre-
vent the dismemberment of the Ottoman
Empire, has steadily progressed along
four main lines of advance ; *viz.*—

1. Siberia to the Far East, where,

for the construction of a line from Victoria Havn
on the Lofoten Fjord in Norway to the head of
the Gulf of Bothnia.   This line was made as far
as the Swedish frontier, and progress was then
stopped.   On March 31st, 1898, the Swedish
Parliament decided by a small majority to proceed
with this railway.   Meanwhile, the Russian lines
in Finland, on the same gauge, were being pressed
on to Torneö, and it has been suggested that
Russia wished to obtain an ice-free port on the
Norwegian seaboard, which at one point is only
twenty miles from the Russian frontier.   If such
a port were obtained, or if the Finnish railway
were prolonged to the Varanger Fjord, the step
would possess little naval importance.

when the seaboard was reached
in the first half of the seventeenth century, support could
be rendered by maritime communications.

2. From the Sea of Aral along the Syr
Daria towards Chimkent (1864),
Tashkent (1865), Kuldja *
(1871), Khokand (1876), and
the Pamirs (1890).

3. Also from the Sea of Aral along
the Amu Daria towards Khiva
(1873) and the southern boundary of Bokhara.†

4. From the Caspian through the
Tekké Turcoman country and
along the Khorassan frontier to
Merv (1884) and Penjdeh (1885).

* Occupied in 1871, but given back to China
by a treaty of February 24th, 1881, in consideration of a payment of nine million roubles.

† The towns of Bokhara and Samarkand were
both occupied from the North in 1868.

It forms no part of the present work to trace the history of the proceedings by which the present gigantic Asiatic dominions of Russia were built up. The processes were those followed by all great Powers in similar circumstances, and notably by Great Britain in India and South Africa. On the second, third, and fourth general lines of advance much fighting occurred, and the natural difficulties arising from the movement of troops over great waterless and sparsely populated districts were necessarily considerable. In achieving the conquest of India, Great Britain had the immense advantage of sea-communications and of operating in a relatively rich country. To maintain her grip upon the Khanates, and to turn them to commercial account, it was absolutely necessary for Russia to undertake railway construction on a vast scale. The

Central Asian Railway (see Map I.), running from the Caspian to Tashkent, a distance of about nine hundred miles, was, therefore, begun in 1880, and completed in 1896.* Like all other railways, this line is capable, as far as its many defects permit, of employment for purely military purposes. Unlike some railways, it is essential for the commercial development of the regions through which it passes, and if it had not been constructed, the expenses of holding and administering these once lawless territories would be enormous.†

From the point of view of Russian sea-power and maritime expansion, the proceedings in the Far East assume

---

* A prolongation of this line to Kuldja, and thence through the heart of Mongolia to Peking, is said to be contemplated; but the latter extension must be deferred for many years.

† Of this our own experience in Uganda gives some indication.

direct importance.   Here the purely
military difficulties have been compara-
tively small ; but the vast distances, the
rigorous climate, and the poverty of
the country have combined to retard
the accomplishment of long-existent
ambitions.   A great maritime and commercial Power, such as Great Britain,
if established in the Far East at the
end of the seventeenth century, would
have expanded its territory Southward
at a speed impossible to Russia.*

The Power now apparently regarded
as a modern interloper in Far Eastern
affairs established a settlement on the
Sea of Okhotsk in 1638, four years
before the outbreak of the Civil War
in England, and concluded with China
the important boundary Treaty of

* Canada did not become an unquestioned
British possession till 1763, and no settlement was
formed in Australasia till 1788.

Nerchinsk in 1689, sixty-eight years before the East India Company occupied Bengal as the result of Plassey. The Amur was reached by Cossacks from Yakutsk in 1644; but subsequent expeditions encountered hostility, and the Chinese, alarmed by the Russian proceedings, sent a considerable force into the territory North of the river. The treaty of 1689, reaffirmed in 1727, fixed a frontier following the Argun and the Stanovai Mountains to the Sea of Okhotsk. This frontier seems to have remained fairly intact for many years; but the importance of the waterway of the Amur naturally attracted the attention of the Russians, and Count Mouravieff, when appointed Governor of Eastern Siberia in 1847, initiated further explorations.* In 1851, Niko-

* *The Russians on the Amur*, E. G. Ravenstein, F.R.G.S., 1861.

laievsk, at the mouth of the river, and Mariinsk " were founded . . . to serve as trading posts for the Russo-American company." *

The ineffective naval operations of the Allies in the North Pacific in 1854-55 gave a fresh impulse to Russian activity. The ports of Kamtschatka and Nikolaievsk on the fifty-fourth parallel of latitude were of little value for naval or commercial purposes, and an extension to the South was inevitable. By a " Treaty of friendship and boundaries," signed on May 16th, 1858, the Amur became the frontier, and the region between the Usuri and the sea was stated to be held in common by Russia and China.† Two years later, by another Treaty signed at Peking on November 14th, 1860, the Usuri became

* *The Russians on the Amur*, E. G. Ravenstein, F.R.G.S., 1861.

† *China Treaties*, Sir E. Hertslet, K.C.B., 1896.

the mutual boundary, and Vladivostock
could be made the naval port of Russia
in the Far East.

The frontier thus established has remained practically unchanged till the
present year. Partially ice-locked, largely
dependent for food on sea-borne supplies,
and separated from European Russia by
immense distances of land and sea, the
former almost impracticable and the
latter certain to be cut in any war with
a great naval Power, the position of
Vladivostock was eminently unsatis-
factory. It was the only vulnerable
point of the Russian Empire in the
event of a war with Great Britain or
France. The opinion of Sir Charles
Dilke, expressed in 1890, that "the
policy which exhausted Russia in the
Crimea"* could be reapplied with equal
success at Vladivostock was evidently

* *Problems of Greater Britain*, 1890.

unfounded, since the difficulties of communication which rendered the position insecure would have effectually prevented the exhaustion of her European forces, which could not be brought into play. On the other hand, the perfectly correct view that Russia, if challenged, " must fight at Vladivostock, while she would fight at a great disadvantage,"* had long been understood by Russian soldiers and statesmen. To remove this obvious source of weakness, and to render Vladivostock secure against a powerful oversea attack, one measure alone could suffice. Railway communication with European Russia must be established at all cost, and the gigantic project of the trans-Siberian line was begun in 1891, and has since been carried on with vigour and success. (See Map I.) Vladivostock, in railway communication

* *Problems of Greater Britain,* 1890.

with the heart of Russia, would cease to be a palpably vulnerable point in her armour, but would retain great disabilities as a naval and commercial harbour.

A warm-water port in the Far East, such as Great Britain obtained in 1842, was, therefore, essential to Russian development, long retarded; and in view of the astonishing naval progress of Japan, such a port became an object of special desire, recognised by British statesmen. The long line of the Siberian railway completely overlaps the north of Manchuria. (See Map II.) Considerable military forces were concentrated at Vladivostock and echeloned along the Usuri and Amur.* It had long been obvious that, in the event of any

* The field troops in Eastern Siberia at the beginning of the present year consisted of thirty-eight squadrons, seventeen batteries of artillery, and thirty-seven infantry battalions. These numbers have since been somewhat increased.

symptoms of the break-up of China, Manchuria would at once pass under Russian control, unless any Power was able and willing to offer armed opposition. No study of history or grasp of strategic principles was needed for the clear understanding of the significance of the anxiety displayed by Russia when the Japanese overran the Liao-tong Peninsula in 1895. The French Alliance was at once invoked to secure the evacuation of this desirable territory, and Germany, with ulterior objects of her own, joined in bringing direct pressure to bear upon the Government of the Mikado. Henceforth it was patent to the least instructed observer that Manchuria was ear-marked. The assertion of a sphere of influence, protectorate, usufruct, or possession—the terms in some circumstances are synonymous—was now only a question of time.

In 1896, a concession was obtained to cut off the great northerly bend of the Siberian railway by carrying a line across Manchuria. (See Maps.) The German occupation of Kiao-chau, accompanied by hinterland concessions, served as a signal. The sanctity of northern Chinese territory was at length violated by a European Power, and the ports of the Liao-tong Peninsula could at once be occupied by Russia.

Addressing the Primrose League,* Lord Salisbury said : " I think Russia has made a great mistake in taking Port Arthur. I do not think it is any use to her whatever." There is probably no naval or military officer in this or in any other country who would agree with this opinion. Russia is in the habit of taking no step without an exhaustive study of the naval and

* Albert Hall, May 4th, 1898.

military conditions involved. In such
matters, Russia does not make mistakes,
as her history abundantly proves. For
the moment Port Arthur and Ta-lien-
wan * are no sources of strength. In
less than ten years the Russian position
in Manchuria will be unassailable, and
Port Arthur, having regard to its geographical position, will be quite as
strong as Cronstadt or Sebastopol. In
substituting Port Arthur for Vladivostock as her principal naval station in
the Far East, Russia gains immense
advantages. The latter has scanty

---

* Judging from the China correspondence, the
astonishing illusion that Russia required only a
commercial port in the Liao-tong Peninsula seems
to have been cherished, and the discovery that a
naval station was to be created seems to have come
as a surprise. In the British Empire, however,
naval and commercial ports are either combined,
as at Hong-kong and Singapore, or in close
juxtaposition, as at the Cape.

local resources, and is practically an island dependent on an uncompleted single line of railway four thousand four hundred miles in length for its communications, being thus far less favourably circumstanced than Hong-kong, in the hands of a great naval and maritime Power. The former possesses coal, iron, rich agricultural possibilities, and a hardy population of four millions, capable of furnishing excellent military material. It is also easily defensible against naval attack; and with a railway and a well-organised army at its back, it will have nothing to fear from operations such as those of the Crimean campaign, undertaken by a European Power at a vast distance from any home base. Finally, when the Manchurian railways are constructed, great military forces will be within striking distance of Peking. (See

Map II.) No territorial advance of Russia in the present century is comparable in importance to the step which has just been taken, after long and careful preparation.

The naval position of Russia is absolutely unique. Throughout the long struggle between France and Great Britain, plans for a combination of the Brest and Toulon fleets formed a dominant feature of French strategy. Brest and Toulon are, however, only eighteen hundred miles apart, and the former projects boldly into the Atlantic. The centres of Russian sea-power are in the Gulf of Finland, the Black Sea, and the Far East. The distance from the Neva to Sebastopol is about four thousand eight hundred miles, and from Sebastopol to Port Arthur about nine thousand miles. Powerful squadrons are maintained in the Baltic and Black

Sea,* and the fleet in the Far East varies in strength according to political exigencies. This fleet at present consists of—

Battle-ships	...	...	...	2 †
First-class cruisers ...	...	...	7
Second-class cruisers	...	...	2
Gunboats ...	...	...	...	6
Torpedo gunboats ...	...	...	2

This is the largest force ever maintained by Russia in the Pacific, and it will doubtless be increased in the near future. In addition to the above, there is a small squadron in the Mediterranean, at present consisting of—

Battle-ships	...	...	...	2 ‡
Gunboats ...	...	...	...	2
Torpedo gunboat	...	...	1
Sea-going torpedo-boats	...	...	2

---

* See pp. 114 and 115.

† *Navarin* and *Sissoi Veliky* (*Naval Annual,* 1898).

‡ *Alexander II.* and *Nicolai I.*, belonging to the Baltic squadron (*Naval Annual,* 1898).

The Russian naval stations are as follows :—

Baltic—First class : Cronstadt, St. Petersburg.
Second class : Revel, Sveaborg, Port Alexander III. at Libau.*
Black Sea—First class : Nicolaieff.
Second class : Sebastopol, Batoum.
Pacific—Second class : Vladivostock.
(Port Arthur, Ta-lien-wan.)
Caspian—Minor : Astrabad, Baku.

In peace-time, the redistribution of naval force can be arranged without any difficulty by the aid of foreign ports, and the successive reinforcements and reliefs of the Russian squadron in the Far East have been facilitated by the British coaling stations of Aden, Colombo, Singapore, and Hong-kong. In war, all great movements depend on coal available in convenient harbours or carried by colliers. By the superior naval Power, if its geographical con-

* New "advanced base" in open waters (*Naval Annual*, 1898).

ditions are favourable, coaling arrangements can generally be made which impose no serious restrictions on strategic combinations. In this respect, however, Russia is placed at a manifest disadvantage. Not only are the distances which separate her naval stations enormous, but the exits from the Baltic and Black Sea are cramped and easily watched, while the Suez Canal is an additional source of danger.

The powerful Baltic and Black Sea fleets, backed by the whole of the military resources of Russia, which, by means of railways, can be rapidly brought to bear on any threatened portion of the seaboard, render Russia practically unassailable in these two seas. Adequate naval force would enable a blockade of either to be maintained; but a hostile squadron could obtain no results of importance, and military operations,

such as those carried on in 1854-55, are
now impossible, unless combined with
successful invasion across the land frontier. The geographical disadvantages
of Russia in regard to offensive operations contribute powerfully to her
security against sea-borne attacks. In
the Far East, her position has hitherto
materially differed. Better placed for
offensive operations, she has been at
the same time more easily assailable.
Vladivostock, as has been pointed out,
is not only isolated, but extremely poor
in local resources, and it may be doubted
whether the long Siberian railway could
have successfully competed with maritime communications in the accumulation
and the maintenance of the forces by
which the issue would be determined.
The development of the resources of
Manchuria will effect a great consolidation of Russian strength in the Far

East. Here, as now in the Baltic and
the Black Sea, she will in a few years
be practically unassailable.

Russian naval policy from the time of
the Crimean War to 1882 appears to
have been defensive. The number of
coast-defence craft built was large, and
the navy was regarded primarily as a
guarantee of the security of the seaboard. Partly on account of the strong
antagonism shown by British Governments, more especially in 1877-78, and
partly as a corollary of the general
progress of the nation, this policy has
undergone modification. In the great
efforts made since 1882, and in the
extensive programme recently adopted,*
the desire to enable the navy to assume
an offensive *rôle* in war is manifest.
The Russian mercantile marine is small,
and shows no signs of marked increase;

* See pp. 116 and 117.

the commercial interests at stake on the high seas are relatively moderate.* The war navy is, however, being steadily developed, and such ships as the *Rurik*, *Rossia*, and *Gromoboy*, as well as the so-called " Volunteer Fleet," are clearly intended to attack an enemy's commerce. British writers are never tired of asserting that our splendid Navy cannot possibly be regarded in the light of a menace to other nations, since it is a necessity arising out of the conditions of our imperial existence. Foreign Powers cannot be expected to see the matter in the same light ; and to Russians, remembering 1854-55 and 1878, British sea-power does unquestionably appear in a threatening aspect.

In a war with Great Britain the Russian navy would undoubtedly be neutralised, and reinforcements or com-

* See p. 130.

binations between the naval centres would be impossible. In the Far East, however, it might be practicable, especially at the outset of hostilities, to act with some effect against British commerce. Here, therefore, the *Rossia*, *Rurik* (Fig. 4), *Pamyat Azova* (Fig. 3), with four other first-class cruisers, are to be found, and it is intended within two years to station six fast ships belonging to the Volunteer Fleet in these waters. An alliance with a European naval Power able to occupy the British squadrons would materially alter the situation, and might provide the Russian battle-ship squadrons with opportunities for offensive action. The French fleet, with its bases in the Atlantic and the Mediterranean, was thus a prize worth playing for, and the Franco-Russian understanding must necessarily be regarded as an attempt

to create a counterpoise to British sea-
power, rather than as a combination
directed against the Triple Alliance
now fallen into decrepitude. The rapid
growth of the French and Russian
navies has, therefore, stimulated further
efforts in this country. It has been
laid down as a principle of policy that
our fleet must be enabled to meet those
of the two greatest naval Powers, and
in present circumstances the costly com-
petition must apparently proceed.

Meanwhile, other States are develop-
ing marked naval activity. Germany
has recently decided upon great aug-
mentations to her fleet, which is to be
enabled to operate as a powerful compact force in the Baltic and North Sea,
and to afford protection to her rapidly
growing commerce. The formidable
fleet of Japan, based upon its home
ports, may be said to hold the balance

of naval power in the Far East. The war now in progress will inevitably lead to a great development of the navy of the United States. There is every sign that sea-power will play an even greater part in the future than it has in the past, while the complexity of the naval situation has never been so great as now. In the case of Russia, however, geographical disadvantages must apparently remain, and her fleet, even if greatly increased, cannot hope to play the great *rôle* on the high seas which is possible to the forces of Great Britain, of France, and of the United States.

All the European squadrons—British, French, Russian, and German—in the Far East would in the event of war suffer from the great distance of their primary bases. Great Britain, holding an unrivalled chain of stations on the routes to the China Seas, and having in Hong-kong an important source of supply and means of refitting, possesses evident advantages; but, now as always, the difficulties of carrying on naval war increase with the distance from the central sources of national strength. On the other hand, Japan, with well-equipped dockyards and a powerful and highly organised army, is on the spot. Between Russia and Japan there is an evident divergence of interests and a clashing of ambitions, which sooner or later may lead to war.

The Japanese fleet, built and building, consists of * :—

	No.	Tonnage.
Battle-ships ...	8	101,630
Armoured cruisers ...	11	68,696
Protected cruisers ...	23	81,670

together with 16 unprotected cruisers and torpedo gunboats, 11 destroyers, and 150 torpedo-boats.

* *The Naval Pocket Book*, 1898.

This, in the hands of an eminently fighting people possessing great naval aptitudes, is an extremely formidable force, and the readiness of Russia to come to an understanding with Japan in regard to Korea is easily understood. The Japanese menace in the Far East, apart from any fear of the action of Great Britain, would suffice to induce Russia to seek a strong naval alliance, and to strain every effort to increase her power in the China Seas. It must, therefore, be her policy to render her Pacific squadron self-supporting as far as possible, and this was impracticable while Vladivostock remained the naval base. In possession of the Liao-tong Peninsula, with the large resources of Manchuria and railway communication at its back, Russia may be able to render her squadron in the Far East independent of the support of

European bases in war. The task will
require time and great expenditure ;
but we may be certain that it will be
undertaken with energy and ability.

CHAPTER IX.

ANGLO-RUSSIAN RELATIONS.

DURING the last half of the present century, the relations between Russia and Great Britain have profoundly influenced international politics. Those relations will present a perplexing problem to future historians. When the territories of two great Powers are separated by a vast tract of country offering no marked physical barriers, and sparsely populated by nomad tribes or uncivilised states mutually hostile, stability of frontier is impossible. One or both of the great Powers must inevitably advance, absorbing the inter-

vening territory, until the two Powers
come into contact at some boundary
established by treaty and formally
delimitated. The history of the world
shows that a strong and a progressive
Power, unrestrained by any great
natural boundary, will always expand
into the territory of uncivilised and
unhomogeneous neighbours. The great
empires of the Old and of the Modern
World have been thus created. The
force of inevitable natural expansion is
something quite apart from, and slower
but more certain in its action than, such
great waves of invasion as that of the
Tartars which almost engulfed Russia
in the thirteenth century. To the
operation of this force, the consolidation
of the United States, of our Indian
Empire, and of Canada is due. In
Africa, the process is still going on;
but the end is near at hand, since the

expanding Powers are now nearly in contact at all points.

At the beginning of this century, when Russia was pressing back the Persian frontier and aiming at the command of the Caspian Sea, Great Britain had absorbed Bengal and moved westward along the line of the Ganges beyond Delhi. Central and Western India were still independent. Henceforth the spheres of influence of the two great Powers steadily and inevitably tended to approach, the expansion of Great Britain proceeding at much greater speed than that of her rival. The annexation of the Punjab by Lord Dalhousie in 1849 "carried our territorial frontier across the Indus right up to the base of the Afghan hills, finally extinguished the long rivalry of the native Indian powers, and absorbed under our sovereignty the last kingdom that remained outside the pale of British Empire in India."* By this time Russia had subdued the Southern Kirghiz and founded Kopal, near the frontier of the Chinese province of Kuldja; but the advance from the Caspian through the Tekké country towards Herat had scarcely commenced, and Khiva, only two hundred miles from the Sea of Aral, was not taken till 1873. Lord Auckland's ill-judged interference in the affairs of Afghanistan in 1838 had, however, been inspired by the dawning fear of Russian progress, and was the outward and visible sign of a new departure in British policy. "What did this new departure imply? Not that we had any quarrel with the Afghans, from whom we were separated by the five rivers whose floods unite in the Indus. It

* *Rise of the British Dominion in India*, Sir Alfred Lyall, K.C.B.

meant that, after half a century's respite, the English were again coming into contact with a rival European influence on Asiatic ground."*

Whether, if Lord Auckland's schemes had not ended in disastrous failure, Great Britain would have over-stepped the gigantic natural boundary of the Hindu-Kush to meet her rival on the banks of the Oxus, or strayed onwards from Herat to the sparse oases of Southern Turkestan, we cannot now know. Such movements would have been unwise to the last degree, and could have resulted only in weakening our position. The "forward policy" of 1838 was, however, checked by military failure attended with grave loss of prestige, and could not be revived till a later date. Meanwhile, Great Britain had reached, recognised, and

* *Rise of the British Dominion in India.*

been compelled to recoil from a great natural boundary from which Russia was still distant.

From this period two main ideas seem to have possessed British imagination and inspired British policy.* In the first place, the visionary schemes of the invasion of India which were suggested to Peter the Great and to Catharine, and resubmitted by Napoleon, for purposes of his own, to Paul and to Alexander I., came to be seriously regarded, and the British people were led to believe that the conquest of India was the main object of Russian ambition. In the second place, it seems to have been thought that the inevitable expansion of a great Power, regarded as inconvenient, could be arrested by diplomatic activity in

---

* Both have been ineffectually combated by individual writers at various times.

regions where Great Britain had no *locus standi* of any kind—regions which we did not desire to occupy, but which were to be kept in a state of perpetual barbarism by a copious use of paper.

The spurious will of Peter the Great may have played a part in misguiding public opinion, for which purpose it was intended. It is probable that the majority of Englishmen believe that the main object of this document was to enjoin upon Russia the invasion of India. As a matter of fact India is mentioned only in Clause VIII., which runs as follows:—

Bear in mind that the commerce of India is the commerce of the world, and that he who controls it is the dictator of Europe; no occasion should therefore be lost to provoke war with Persia, to hasten her decay, to advance to the Persian Gulf, and then to endeavour to re-establish the ancient trade of the Levant through Syria.

The preceding clause inculcates close alliance with this country :—

Enter into a close alliance with England, and maintain direct relations with her by means of a good commercial treaty ; allow her even to exercise a certain monopoly in the interior of the State, so that a good understanding may by degrees be established between the English merchants and sailors and ours, who on their part are in favour of everything which tends to perfect and increase the Russian navy.

As this will was written to Napoleon's order at a time when he was preparing to invade Russia with a promiscuous army of four hundred and fifty thousand men composed of most European nationalities, it is natural that the main object should have been to excite fears of Russian aggression among the Continental peoples. Accordingly the so-called will urges Russia to push " her regular troops to the Rhine," and " follow them up with the hordes of Asia."

Other hordes were to embark in the Sea
of Azof and at Archangel to "inundate
Italy, Spain, and France," to "plunder
a portion of the inhabitants, carry off
others into slavery to re-people the
deserts of Siberia, and render the remainder incapable of escaping our yoke."
Clearly it might be expected that M.
Lesur's ingenious fabrication would have
powerfully impressed the imaginations
of Germans, Frenchmen, Italians, and
Spaniards.   By a curious freak of circumstance, Great Britain—who is not
threatened—has alone been impressed,
and Napoleon's scheme has succeeded
as he could not have expected.

The early projects for the invasion of
India were framed in days when geo-
graphy was in its infancy, and when
fabulous stories of the wealth of Hindu-
stan gained easy credence—in days also
when British power was limited to a

footing on the seaboard. All is now changed, and British power in Asia has attained to a degree of consolidation permanently denied to that of Russia. Large numbers of able books and official memoranda have been written on the defence of the Indian frontier, but no one has yet attempted to make a reasoned study of the means and the methods by which invasion could be attempted. So long as the command of the sea can be held, and the loyalty of the native army and of the mass of the peoples of India can be counted upon, invasion is out of the question ; but our extreme anxiety in regard to the security of the strongest frontier in the world has supplied Russia with a lever the use of which she well understands.

The policy—persistently followed— of attempting to stem the Russian advance in Central Asia by diplomatic notes baffles explanation. An island people, unaccustomed to the idea of sharing a frontier with a great Power, may have caught at the fallacy that the operations of natural forces can be arrested by mere protests; but in our dealings with France in regard to African territory there is no parallel to the treatment accorded to Russia. In the one case, the claim to exclude a rival from regions which we had no intention of ever occupying has never been set up; in the other case, this claim has for many years been the dominant note of our foreign policy. The literature dealing with this subject is various, extensive, and amazing. There is no record of any Russian remonstrance against the British annexation of the Punjab; but when, in 1869, Russia occupied Krasnovodsk, a port on the eastern shore of the Caspian about twelve hundred miles

in a direct line from Peschawur, we
are told that " the British Ambassador
at St. Petersburg at once demanded
explanations,"* and this instance is
typical of the long series of diplomatic
proceedings which culminate in the
China papers recently published. Remonstrance against each successive step
taken by Russia in regions where we
have no substantial interests present or
prospective appears to have grown into
an established tradition. A habit once
acquired escapes self-criticism, and even
its humorous side may elude observation. While continuously protesting
against the Russian occupation of territories which we do not desire, we have,
since 1884 only, annexed or brought
under our influence no less than
2,600,000 square miles † of the earth's

* *Russia's March towards India,* 1894.
† Lord Rosebery, Edinburgh, October 9th, 1896.

surface, increasing the sum-total of British territory by about one-third. Moreover, the diplomatic campaign waged against Russia has no parallel in our dealings with other Powers, which have meanwhile annexed territory in which we had direct interests. While Russia could not occupy the remote oasis of Merv without arousing great irritation, France might annex Tunis and Madagascar without even exciting mild surprise.

On the other hand, the Russian policy has been almost equally inexplicable. Each British protest has been met by an explanation or an assurance alike absolutely and obviously valueless, so long as the natural forces of expansion were still in full operation and the mutual frontier remained to be reached. A weakness for *finesse* may perhaps have led Russian statesmen to a course from which they

could reap no real advantage. France
or Germany in similar circumstances
would have politely but firmly declined
to entertain any protest in relation to
territory to which Great Britain could
show no claim. If Russia had from
the first taken this line, both nations
would have benefited, and the charges
of faithlessness which have been brought
against her would have been averted.

When once the idea took root that it
was the principal object of British policy
to thwart Russian aspirations in every
way open to diplomacy, counter-moves
at all parts of the international chess-
board were certain to be made. It is
impossible to justify the action of
Russia in Bulgaria in 1885-86, her
attitude in regard to the Armenian
atrocities, or her behaviour during and
after the Greek crisis ; but, with
governments, as with individuals, the

moral sense is apt to be blunted by ill-temper.

Other results have followed from the antagonism which our policy has directly provoked. Since 1878 there has been a marked diminution of Russian trade with Great Britain. The figures, as nearly as they can be obtained, are :—

YEAR.	IMPORTS.	EXPORTS.*	TOTAL.
1878	£16,157,000	19,111,000	35,268,000
1896	11,131,000	16,090,000	27,221,000

The fall is greatest in imports, and it is probably not unconnected with political sentiment, which in the ship-building trade especially has operated to the disadvantage of British industry.

Whether the plain lessons of the past have even now been taken to heart in this country is doubtful. The policy of free ports in the Far East, which

* Of Russian exports to Great Britain, wheat and other grain account for the greater part.

we have proclaimed solely because it is believed to promise us the *maximum* of advantage with the *minimum* of responsibility, seems already to be regarded as invested with divine sanctions. This policy is practicable only by agreement with other Powers, or by our assumption of a protectorate over the whole of China. Such agreement is impossible, because other Powers are the interpreters of their individual interests, which, rightly or wrongly, they regard as different from our own. Great Britain is not prepared to assert a protectorate over China, and to accept the immense responsibilities entailed. She has, however, an absolute right to define her sphere of influence, to secure within it the application of the doctrine of free ports, to treat violation of this sphere as a *casus belli*, and to prepare to defend it if the need arises.

This is a practical and an intelligible policy which awaits realisation. Natural laws will continue to fulfil themselves in spite of Foreign Offices, and in China, as in Central Asia, Russia will continue to advance till she is stopped by a delimitated frontier marking the territory in the occupation or under the direct protectorate of a great Power able and ready to assert its just rights, if necessary, by war. Till this condition is reached, equilibrium will not be established. If the British people can be made to understand that the frontiers of a world-wide empire must sooner of later march with those of rivals, and that " buffer States " cannot be maintained except by mutual agreement between the Powers whose territories they separate, our international relations will be placed on a sounder and a more dignified footing.

In political questions of this nature views must differ ; but there are certain pregnant facts which no sophistry can obscure and no thoughtful student of recent history can deny. From first to last the policy of hostility to Russia has proved an absolute failure. It has not in the slightest degree retarded her Asiatic expansion. It has bred and maintained misunderstanding and ill-feeling between two great nations. It has directly provoked measures of reprisal, which have entailed commercial and other loss upon the people of Great Britain and of India. It has not conduced to our national dignity. Its drift is towards war upon some minor issue, such as that of Penjdeh, which experts alone could pretend to understand—war from which no national advantage could be obtained. If it could be finally buried in oblivion, Europe, as well as Great Britain, would be a gainer.

Reflection will show that, even after two centuries of expansion, Russia has not occupied a square yard of territory which is now or has ever been desired by Great Britain. This cannot be said of France, of Germany, or of the United States. In such circumstances, it is specially difficult to believe that a direct understanding with Russia in Asia—such an understanding as was reached with Germany in East Africa and in New Guinea, and as we are patiently seeking to obtain with France in West Africa—is impossible. Until Russia advances into a defined sphere of British influence, we have no grievance against her; until such a sphere is defined, we have no claim to arrest her advance. No policy is so dangerous as that of drift; no assumption is so gratuitous as that Russia is "our great enemy." *   To remove the long-standing antagonism between the two nations, and to substitute direct agreements between London and St. Petersburg for competitive manipulations of the dummy Government at Peking, would be a task worthy of a great statesman, and a powerful guarantee of the peace of the world.

* *The Balance of Power*, 1888.

INDEX.

THE RUSSIAN EMPIRE

London, John Murray, Albemarle Street.

MANCHURIA

FIVE YEARS IN SIAM:

A Record of Journeys and of Life among the People
from 1891 to 1896.

By H. WARINGTON SMYTH, M.A., LL.B.,

Formerly Director of the Department of Mines in Siam.

With Illustrations from the Author's Drawings and Maps. 2 vols.
Crown 8vo. Price 24s.

"Mr. Smyth possesses also many of the mental qualities which go to
make a good traveller, or at least a good writer of books of travel."—*Times.*
"A deeply interesting account of the Siamese people, their ways, their
views, and their country."—*Daily Chronicle.*
"Here at last is the kind of book for which all English readers interested
in Siam have been waiting. It is the work of a writer whose conclusions
are the result of personal observation."—*Daily News.*

THE RISE AND EXPANSION OF THE BRITISH DOMINION IN INDIA.

From the Early Days of the East India Company
to the Mutiny.

By SIR ALFRED LYALL, G.C.B.

A New Library Edition, with Considerable Additions. With
Coloured Maps. 8vo. Price 12s. net.

A MANUAL OF NAVAL ARCHITECTURE.

For the Use of Officers of the Navy, the Mercantile
Marine, Ship-Owners, Ship-Builders,
and Yachtsmen.

By SIR W. H. WHITE, K.C.B., F.R.S.

Third Edition, thoroughly Revised and in great part Rewritten.
With 176 Illustrations. Medium 8vo. Price 24s.

HANDBOOK FOR INDIA AND CEYLON.

With 50 Maps and Plans. An entirely new and compact Guide
for the whole of India and Ceylon. Thoroughly revised. Price 20s.

HANDBOOK FOR JAPAN.

By BASIL HALL CHAMBERLAIN and W. B. MASON.

Third Edition. With 10 Maps and a Plan of the Buddhist and
Shinto Temples of Ikegami and Izumo. Price 20s.

JOHN MURRAY, ALBEMARLE STREET.